Economic Decline in Britain

Economic Decline in Britain

The Shipbuilding Industry, 1890–1970

Edward H. Lorenz

CLARENDON PRESS · OXFORD
1991

Oxford University Press, Walton Street, Oxford OX2 6DP
Oxford New York Toronto
Delhi Bombay Calcutta Madras Karachi
Petaling Java Singapore Hong Kong Tokyo
Nairobi Dar es Salaam Cape Town
Melbourne Auckland
and associated companies in
Berlin Ibadan

Oxford is a trade mark of Oxford University Press

Published in the United States
by Oxford University Press, New York

British Library Cataloguing in Publication Data
Data available

Library of Congress Cataloging in Publication Data
Lorenz, Edward.
Economic decline in Britain: the shipbuilding industry, 1890–1970
/ Edward H. Lorenz.
p. cm.
Revision of the author's thesis (Ph. D.)—Cambridge University.
Includes bibliographical references and index.
1. Shipbuilding industry—Great Britain—History—20th century.
2. Shipbuilding industry—Great Britain—History—19th century.
3. Factory management—Great Britain—History—20th century.
4. Factory management—Great Britain—History—19th century.
5. Industrial relations—Great Britain—History—20th century.
6. Industrial relations—Great Britain—History—19th century.
7. Competition, International. I. Title.
VM299.7.G7L67 1991   338.4'762382'0941—dc20   91–17188
ISBN 0–19–828502–7

Typeset by Graphicraft Typesetters Ltd., Hong Kong
Printed in Great Britain by
Biddles Ltd,
Guildford & King's Lynn

Acknowledgements

THIS book is a revision of my Cambridge Ph.D. thesis, and my first acknowledgement is to S. F. Wilkinson who supervised my dissertation research at Cambridge between 1978 and 1983. At Wilkinson's recommendation, I investigated differences in work organization between British and French shipbuilding and their relation to national systems of industrial relations. The thesis also contained a short concluding chapter addressing the implications of the argument for industry competitive performance.

The catalyst for transforming the thesis into a book about British competitive decline came in 1983, when Patrick O'Brien agreed to review the text for Oxford University Press. O'Brien suggested that the manuscript contained the elements of a novel explanation for British shipbuilding decline, and he encouraged me to amplify the argument and provide further empirical support. He also made what proved to be a most intelligent suggestion, that I consider the relevance of evolutionary economic modelling, associated notably with Richard Nelson and Sidney Winter, in my explanation for decline.

Progress on the manuscript was halted in the autumn of 1983 by my appointment as Economic and Social Research Council Postdoctoral Fellow at the Department of Applied Economics at Cambridge. My three-year tenure at the DAE was almost entirely devoted to initiating, and conducting field-work for, a new project concerning contemporary changes in industrial structure and competitive performance in British and French manufacturing. With my appointment as Assistant Professor of Economics at the University of Notre Dame in 1986, teaching and administrative responsibilities precluded my giving the manuscript any serious attention until 1988.

Most of Chapter 1 and the basic argument about British shipbuilding decline in Chapter 5 were worked out during the summer of 1989 while a Visiting Scholar at the Minda de Gunzburg Center for European Studies at Harvard University. At this time, Diego Gambetta of King's College, Cambridge read these chapters and persuaded me that they comprised the elements of a theory of economic decline. He encouraged me to state the argument precisely and in general terms. Chapter 6 is the result of these endeavours. Most of what is of value in Chapter 6 is due to Gambetta, without whom the level of argument would have been much lower. The final revisions to the manuscript were completed early in 1990 while a Visiting Scholar at the Sloan School of Management at MIT.

A number of friends and colleagues commented on portions of the manuscript or on conference papers drawn from it. My thanks go to Terry Aladjem, Gerry Berk, Amitava Dutt, Bernie Elbaum, Victor Goldberg, David Hachen, Wayne Lewchuk, Cristina Marcuzzo, Donald McCloskey, Jim McGoldrick, Joseph Melling, Phillip Mirowski, Daniel Nelson, Patrick O'Brien, Alistair Reid, Jill Rubery, Paul Ryan, Steven Tolliday, Paola Villa, Frank Wilkinson, and Jonathan Zeitlin.

Campbell McMurray, Archivist at the National Maritime Museum at Greenwich, gave invaluable assistance in using the records of the Shipbuilding Employers' Federation. Martin Stopford, of British Shipbuilders at Newcastle-upon-Tyne, provided me with useful documentation on post-World War II conditions in British shipbuilding. The École Normale Superiéure was kind enough to allow me to spend a year there as an *auditeur étranger* while conducting research on the French shipbuilding industry.

I would also like to thank N. Rowena Anketell and Juanita Potter for a thorough job of copy-editing, and Andrew Schuller of Oxford University Press for his unwavering encouragement during the book's long gestation.

I am grateful to the editors of the *Journal of European Economic History* and the *Mouvement social* for permission to reprint extracts of the following articles: 'Two Patterns of Development: The Labour Process in the British and French Shipbuilding Industries 1880 to 1930', *Journal of European Economic History*, 13: 3 (winter 1984); and 'L'Offre de travail et les strategies d'emploi dans la construction navale en France et en Grande-Bretagne (1890–1970)', *Mouvement social*, 138 (Jan.–Mar. 1987). I would like to thank the editors of Oxford University Press for allowing me to reprint extracts from E. H. Lorenz and F. Wilkinson, 'The Shipbuilding Industry', in B. Elbaum and W. Lazonick (eds.), *The Decline of the British Economy* (Oxford University Press, Oxford, 1986).

E.H.L.

Contents

Abbreviations

AREMORS	Association de recherches et d'études du mouvement ouvrier de la région de Saint-Nazaire
ASB	Amalgamated Society of Boilermakers, Shipwrights, Blacksmiths, and Structural Workers
BESA	British Engineering Standards Association
BETURE	Bureau d'études techniques pour l'urbanisme et l'équipement
ILO	International Labour Organization
INSEE	Institut national de la statistique et des études économiques
NSS	National Shipbuilders Security Ltd.
NUGMW	National Union of General and Municipal Workers
SEF	Shipbuilding Employers' Federation
SITB	Shipbuilding Industry Training Board
SRNA	Shipbuilders' and Repairers' National Association
SSA	Shipconstructors' and Shipwrights' Association

1

Introduction

IRON and steel shipbuilding played an important role in late nineteenth and early twentieth-century British economic development. The value of new merchant vessels accounted for approximately 1.25 per cent of Britain's gross domestic product at the turn of the century, and the industry employed about 2 per cent of the industrial labour force. Between 1890 and 1914 the rate of growth of shipbuilding output exceeded that of the economy as a whole (Pollard and Robertson 1979: 6–7, 30–4).

What is more, shipbuilding was one of the few heavy industries in which Britain maintained undisputed international supremacy in the decade before World War I. Britain accounted for 60 per cent of world output of ships and controlled some 80 per cent of the world export market as late as 1913 (Parkinson, 1956: 242). By the mid-1960s, however, the British shipbuilding industry had been reduced to comparative insignificance, the tonnage produced in British yards averaging 8 per cent of world production. Britain's share of the world export market had declined even more precipitously to some 4 per cent, while over 50 per cent of additions to the United Kingdom registered fleet were being produced abroad. What accounts for the remarkable competitive reversal of this once great industry?

The aims of this book are to provide a persuasive explanation for the competitive decline of the British shipbuilding industry, and to outline a general hypothesis of British economic decline. The ideas about economic decline developed here draw on previous explanations given in the literature, but also incorporate elements from the 'new' institutional economics, primarily the recent work of Richard Nelson and Sidney Winter (1982) and O. E. Williamson (1985), as well as the seminal contribution of Herbert Simon (1957). The analytical tools developed by these authors to explain decision-making under uncertainty hold

Introduction

unexplored promise for addressing the problem of economic decline.

I will critically examine the principal explanations given in the literature for Britain's economic decline and discuss their relation to the argument presented in this book. But first we need to ask: Has Britain really suffered an economic decline?

I. Britain's Economic Decline

Few statements of fact concerning the aggregate performance of the British economy from the late Victorian period to the present time are not open to dispute. For example, earlier literature debated whether the trend-break or climacteric in Britain's nineteenth-century growth rates in industrial productivity occurred in the 1870s or 1890s (Aldcroft 1968: 12–14; Coppock 1956; Richardson 1965: 128). More recent estimates suggest the slowdown occurred during the period 1899–1913 (Matthews *et al.* 1982: 607).[1] Based on these new dates and his downward-revised estimates of productivity growth during Britain's Industrial Revolution, Nick Crafts (1985: 158) has concluded, 'The best guess now seems to be that the long period from the end of the French Wars to the end of the nineteenth century appears as an epoch of a steady trend-growth in productivity in manufacturing.'

Disagreements over the timing of trend-breaks or precise estimates of growth rates are unlikely ever to be resolved. Researchers can only surmount the non-negligible data problems by making assumptions that others can easily, legitimately, question. One general claim, however, which has not been seriously contested, is that Britain sustained an economic decline from the late Victorian period onwards relative to the United States and to its other major competitors on the Continent. One set of figures illustrating the demarcations of this decline is presented in Table 1.1.

In terms of relative productivity growth, Britain performed

---

[1] Matthews *et al.* (1982: 607) estimate that total-factor productivity growth for manufacturing fell from 0.9% p.a. for the period 1873–99 to 0.3% p.a. for the period 1899–1913.

TABLE 1.1. Growth of gross domestic product per man-year in selected countries

Period	Annual %age growth rates					
	UK	USA	Sweden	France	Germany	Japan
1873–99	1.2	1.9	1.5	1.3	1.5	1.1
1899–1913	0.5	1.3	2.1	1.6	1.5	1.8
1913–24	0.3	1.7	0.3	0.8	−0.9	3.2
1924–37	1.0	1.4	1.7	1.4	3.0	2.7
1937–51	1.0	2.3	2.6	1.7	1.0	−1.3
1951–64	2.3	2.5	3.3	4.3	5.1	7.6
1964–73	2.6	1.6	2.7	4.6	4.4	8.4
1873–1951	0.9	1.7	1.7	1.4	1.3	1.4
1951–73	2.4	2.3	3.0	4.4	4.8	7.9
1873–1973	1.2	1.8	1.9	2.0	2.0	2.6

Source: Matthews *et al*. (1982: Table 2.5, p. 31).

poorly for the entire period 1873–1973 as well as for the sub-period 1873–1951.[2] While Britain performed well in historical terms after World War II, productivity growth rates remained considerably below those of its major competitors during this period, with the exception of the United States.[3] As Table 1.2 shows, Britain's relative decline was accompanied by a progressive loss of world-market share for manufacturing exports.

As a number of authors have pointed out, some of this decline was probably unavoidable (Pollard 1989: 48–9; McCloskey 1981: ch. 5). For example, Britain was bound to lose some of its manufacturing export markets after 1870 as Germany and the United States expanded their own manufacturing sectors behind

[2] With respect to absolute levels of labour productivity, the UK level was roughly comparable to that in the USA in 1870, while the levels in Sweden, Germany, and France were approximately 70, 60, and 60% respectively of the UK level. In 1973 the UK level was approximately 60% of the US level, while the levels in Sweden, Germany, and France were approximately 85, 70, and 70% respectively of the US level (Matthews *et al.* 1982: 32).

[3] The same historical and internationally comparative statement applies to Britain's post-World War II national-income growth rates, except the British rate of growth was lower than the US rate (Denison 1968: 236; Prest and Coppock 1982: 193).

TABLE 1.2. Selected countries' share of world exports of manufactures

Year	% based on values in US$ at current prices					
	UK	USA	Sweden	Germany	France	Japan
1881–5	43.0	6.0	1.0	16.0	15.0	0.0
1899	34.5	12.1	0.9	16.6	14.9	1.6
1913	31.8	13.7	1.5	19.9	12.8	2.5
1929	23.8	21.7	1.8	15.5	11.6	4.1
1937	22.3	20.5	2.8	16.5	6.2	7.4
1950	24.6	26.6	2.8	7.0	9.6	3.4
1964	14.0	20.1	3.4	19.5	8.5	8.3
1973	9.1	15.1	3.3	22.3	9.3	13.1

Source: Matthews *et al.* (1982: Table 14.5, 435).

protective barriers. Assuming equal rates of growth of domestic markets, and no change in each country's share of third-country export markets, this in itself would translate into a slower rate of growth for the British economy as a whole.

British industrial performance during the late Victorian and Edwardian periods was far from uniform. In the case of steel, one of Britain's major nineteenth-century staples, there was a progressive loss of export-market share to Germany and the United States. Allen (1979) has presented figures showing that total-factor productivity was lower in British steel before World War I, and Elbaum (1986) has argued that with suitable organizational and technological restructuring the industry could have done better. On the other hand, other major British staples, including shipbuilding and cotton, remained virtually untouched by foreign competition prior to 1914. Certain sectors, such as bicycles and textile machinery, actually increased their share of world export markets during the Edwardian period (Aldcroft 1968: 11–36; Lazonick 1986: 18–19; Pollard 1989: 55–7).

That some decline was unavoidable can be argued with even greater force for the post-World War II period. As Denison (1968: 253–7) has pointed out, productivity growth for the economy as a whole in Germany, France, and Italy benefited from the movement of a large portion of their work-force out of

TABLE 1.3. Differences in growth rates of total-factor productivity, 1950–1962

	Excess over the UK (%age points per annum)			
	USA	France	Germany	Italy
Output per unit of input	0.14	2.19	2.95	3.02
Figures adjusted for the contraction of agriculture and self-employment	−0.5	1.41	2.14	1.86

Source: Denison (1968: 236).

agriculture and self-employment into the higher productivity industrial sectors. Britain, with only about 5 per cent of its labour force in agriculture in 1950, was precluded from benefiting from this type of productivity growth (Denison 1968: 268; Kaldor 1966).[4]

While this constraint provides a partial explanation for Britain's comparatively poor record after World War II, none the less a considerable shortfall in total-factor productivity growth remains unexplained as shown in Table 1.3 above. The dismal picture painted by these aggregate figures is supported by evidence from specific sectors. Table 1.4 shows that while productivity in vehicle manufacturing in Britain compared well with that in Japan or on the Continent during the 1950s, by the early 1970s Britain had fallen behind. Productivity differences in steel were even more pronounced, as Table 1.5 shows.

The shipbuilding industry arguably sustained an even more dramatic decline than that of steel or vehicles. Britain achieved its dominant position in the world shipbuilding market during the period of transition from wooden to iron hull construction between 1860 and 1880. Britain produced on average 75 per cent of

[4] According to Denison (1967: 215) the contribution to national-income growth rates from shifts of resources out of agriculture and self-employment into industry for the period 1950–62 was 1.26, 0.91, 0.88, 0.29, and 0.10% p.a. respectively for Italy, Germany, France, the USA and the UK.

TABLE 1.4. Productivity in vehicle manufacturing in selected countries

	Output of vehicles per employee-year				
	1950	1955	1959	1965	1973
USA	10.0	11.1	10.3	13.9	14.9
UK	3.3	4.2	5.2	5.8	5.1
France	3.2	3.6	5.7	6.1	6.8
West Germany	2.2	3.9	5.6	7.1	7.3
Italy	—	3.0	—	7.4	6.8
Japan	—	1.2	—	4.4	12.2

Source: Pollard (1983: 289).

TABLE 1.5. Steel productivity in selected countries, 1967

Country	Crude-Steel output per man-hour in tons
EEC average	0.107
USA	0.106
Japan	0.081
UK	0.037

Source: Pollard (1982: 294).

world output between 1892 and 1899.[5] Britain's share of the market fell to about 60 per cent around the turn of the century and fluctuated around this level until 1914. This decline resulted from the expansion of shipbuilding capacity in the United States and on the Continent, generally behind protective barriers.[6]

[5] Table A.1. Output figures are derived from *Lloyd's Register of Shipping*, Annual Shipbuilding Returns, unless otherwise stated.

[6] German producers, who offered the British the stiffest competition, built various classes of vessels from the 1890s onwards with little subsidization. They were never successful, however, in making inroads into Britain's control of the cargo section of the market. American builders relied for their commercial orders on legislation requiring lake steamers and coastal vessels to be of domestic manufacture. French builders similarly relied on protective legislation, including the 1881 and 1893 laws which provided subsidies to builders to compensate for customs duties on imported materials. See Charpentier (1945: 183); Pollard (1957: 429–30); Reid (1980: 36); Royal Commission on Depression of Trade, 1886, 3rd Report: (143–53, evidence of J. Price, 186–95, evidence of J. Scott).

TABLE 1.6. Comparisons of labour productivity in shipbuilding, 1900

	Number employed	Tons constructed	Output per head (tons)	No. of firms averaged
UK[a]	85,000	1,290,369	15.2	64
USA	33,340	385,511[b]	11.6	11
Germany	31,310	198,097	6.3	14
France	28,650	134,037	4.7	11

[a] UK firms engaged in naval construction have been excluded, as the output figures provided do not include the displacement tonnage of naval vessels produced.
[b] Includes naval construction of 215,861 displacement tons.

Sources: Numbers employed for the four countries and tons constructed for the UK, USA, and Germany are derived from employment and output figures per firm in Schwartz and von Halle (1902: Tables 36–9, pp. 174–9). Annual tons constructed in France taken from Latty (1951: 236).

Britain's control of the unprotected parts of the export market remained uncontested, its share being 80 per cent as late as 1913.[7]

At the turn of the century, Britain enjoyed a considerable advantage in labour productivity, as shown in Table 1.6.[8] Britain's share of world ship production dropped dramatically during World War I since much of the world market was shut off to British producers. Exports, as a percentage of total British output, dropped from an average of 23.7 per cent during the period

[7] This estimate is based on figures in a study in the *Glasgow Herald* (5 Feb., 1926). See Parkinson (1956: 242). Pollard and Robertson (1979: 43) note that between 1892 and 1913 the tonnage launched in Britain for registration abroad exceeded the total tonnage launched in either Germany or the USA, Britain's two principal competitors.

[8] The British productivity estimate is likely to be upward-biased because the work content per ton produced for a simple cargo vessel is considerably lower than for a sophisticated service vessel or passenger liner. A comparatively large proportion of output in Britain was accounted for by cargo tramps prior to 1914. The US productivity estimate is also biased due to the inclusion of naval construction which is measured in displacement tonnage as opposed to gross tonnage, which is the measure used for merchant construction. Gross tonnage refers to the total volume of a vessel, 1 ton being equivalent to 100 cubic feet, while displacement tonnage is the weight of the water displaced when a ship is fuelled up but empty of cargo and passengers. There is no good way to convert from one measure to the other. See Pollard and Robertson (1979: 237). For further evidence of comparatively high productivity in British shipbuilding at the turn of the century, see Pollard (1957: 438).

TABLE 1.7. Entrances at British ports by %age

Identity of vessels	1913	1929	1937
British	65.8	65.0	55.8
Subsidized foreign[a]	7.5	14.2	17.2
Unsubsidized foreign	26.7	20.8	27.0

[a] Subsidized foreign refers principally to France, Germany, Japan, and the USA.
Source: Sturmey (1962: 127).

1900–13 to an average of 7.8 per cent during the period 1914–18. After the war, during the reconstruction boom, Britain quickly re-established its dominant position, though at a lower level (Cormack, 1930: 308–12). Britain produced on average 45 per cent of world output between 1920 and 1929, and 35 per cent between 1930 and 1939.

The loss of market share during the inter-war years can be attributed in part to protectionist policies abroad. These took a variety of forms, though direct subsidization of shipbuilders was not common. Subsidization was primarily indirect through support to shipping companies. The most common forms of support to owners were postal subventions and direct operating subsidies tied to ship-construction in the home country (Jones 1957: 62–75; Sturmey 1962: ch. 5). Table 1.7 indicates their impact on the competitive position of British operators.[9]

Supply-side factors contributed to Britain's declining market share during the post-1935 boom, as shortages of manpower and

---

[9] The British government belatedly introduced supporting legislation with the British Shipping Act in 1935 which was aimed at the ailing tramp sector of the shipping industry. The legislation provided for a scrap-and-build scheme and a subsidy to tramp owners which varied with the level of freight rates. The subsidy was discontinued in 1937 with the rise in freights. Under the terms of the scrap-and-build scheme owners were to scrap two tons of shipping for each ton built, and ton for ton in the case of assistance received for modernizing vessels. The scheme was little used, at least in part because the subsidy provisions of the act encouraged owners to retain their tonnage while rates were low, and as rates improved there was less incentive to scrap. Only 186,000 gross tons were authorized for construction under the scheme. See Jones (1957: 149–55); Parkinson (1960: 93–4).

TABLE 1.8. Shares of the world export market of selected countries

Period	%age based on tons launched				
	Britain	Japan	Germany	Sweden	France
1948–50	35.0	2.2	0.3	18.3	0.1
1951–5	22.0	10.6	14.9	12.9	2.1
1956–60	6.9	31.6	20.7	12.0	5.8
1961–5	4.5	38.8	13.0	15.7	5.5

Source: Lloyd's Register of Shipping, Annual Shipbuilding Returns.

materials in Britain led to the placement of orders abroad and to a loss of export markets. Imports, which averaged 2.4 per cent for 1920 to 1935, increased to 15.3 per cent in 1936 and 16 per cent in 1938. Holland and Germany were the major exporters to British account. Both Germany and Sweden made significant inroads into foreign markets after 1935, both emerging as major exporters to Norwegian account (Jones 1957: 75–6, 88). Britain's share of the world shipbuilding export market declined from over 40 per cent during the period 1927–30 to 21 per cent for the period 1936–8 (Parkinson 1956: 242).

In contrast to the slow decline of the depressed inter-war period, Britain's market share fell sharply during the post-World War II boom. The more than twofold increase in world output of the 1950s saw the proportion of ships built in Britain cut to 15 per cent. During the 1960s, while world demand expanded at an unprecedented rate, the British industry sustained an absolute decline, with the closure of a number of the major shipyards (Geddes Report 1965–6).

As shown in Table 1.8, the decline in Britain's share of the world export market was equally precipitous, plummeting from 35 per cent in the period 1948–50 to 4.5 per cent in the period 1961–5. Import penetration followed closely on the heels of export-market loss, as British owners responded to the lower prices and quicker delivery dates being offered abroad. As shown in Table 1.9, foreign producers increased their share of the tonnage delivered to the United Kingdom fleet from a paltry 3.2 per

TABLE 1.9. Ships delivered to the United Kingdom's registered fleet

Period	% age based on tons launched from	
	UK yards	Foreign yards
1948–50	100.0	0.0
1951–5	96.8	3.2
1956–60	81.1	19.9
1961–5	61.7	38.3
1966–70	26.0	74.0

Source: Lloyd's Register of Shipping, Annual
Shipbuilding Returns.

cent in the period 1951–5 to 38.3 per cent in the period 1961–5,
and to an overwhelming 74 per cent in the period 1966–70.

By the 1960s, as shown in Table 1.10, there was a considerable
shortfall in labour productivity in Britain as compared with her
principal competitors.[10]

Why was there such a dramatic competitive reversal of this
once great industry? Before providing an answer to this question,
let us make an excursion onto the terrain of general explanations
for Britain's relative economic decline.

II. Explanations for Relative Decline

In the literature on Britain's relative economic decline two basic
explanations can be identified. The first argues that culturally

---

[10] See the Patton Report (1962: 15) which makes clear the comparatively low
productivity of capital in British shipbuilding as compared with Continental
producers.

TABLE 1.10. Comparisons of labour productivity in shipbuilding, 1960–65

Country	Average man-hours per weighted steel ton for 1960–5[a]
Japan	70
Sweden	82
West Germany	155
UK	187

[a] Tonnage figures are weighted to reflect the approximate work content of a vessel. The weights vary from 0.3 for a large tanker to 3.0 for a small service vessel. See Stopford (1988: 310–11).

Source: Alexander and Jenkins (1970: 38).

specific norms or beliefs of British businessmen propelled them into behaviour resulting in various deficiencies in economic performance. This is usually referred to as the entrepreneurial-failure thesis. The second, the rational-choice explanation, denies that business performance was deficient and explains relative decline entirely in terms of the economic and social constraints under which rational decision-makers had to act.

The entrepreneurial-failure thesis has two parts: in the first, cultural norms shape the preferences of the actors, and in the second, culturally specific beliefs affect the way the actors perceive their opportunities. Analyses based on the first part typically argue that the experiences of British businessmen within their culture led them to disparage business activity. The argument goes that resources and talent were progressively diverted to non-business activities to the detriment of competitive performance. This explanation typically takes the form of a three-generation argument as in the following account by Landes (1969: 336):[11]

---

[11] Also see Coleman (1973) and Wiener (1981).

Thus the Britain of the late nineteenth century basked complacently in the sunset of economic hegemony. In many firms, the grandfather who started the business and built it by unremitting application and by thrift bordering on miserliness had long died; the father who took over a solid enterprise and, starting with larger ambitions, raised it to undreamed-of heights, had passed on the reins; now it was the turn of the third generation, the children of affluence, tired of the tedium of trade and flushed with the bucolic aspirations of the country gentleman . . . Many of them retired and forced conversion of their firms into joint-stock companies. Others stayed on and went through the motions of entrepreneurship between long weekends; they worked at play and played at work.

The second part of the entrepreneurial-failure thesis argues that the culturally specific beliefs of the business community led them to make biased estimates of the costs and benefits associated with various options, resulting in lost profitable opportunities. Some years ago Derek Aldcroft argued that Britain's legacy of nineteenth-century industrial dominance led entrepreneurs during the twentieth century to be contemptuous of new techniques or departures from established forms of enterprise organization. The most damning example, perhaps, is their alleged failure to undertake profitable investments in research and in scientific and technical training (Aldcroft 1964: 118):

One of the reasons for the slow progress made in both the old and new industries was the lack of appreciation by industrialists of the importance of science and technology and its application to industry . . . But the fact was that British economic supremacy had been built up by a nation of 'practical tinkers' and British industrialists were strikingly reluctant to depart from 'rule of thumb' methods and seemed even proud of the fact that they carried out little original research or employed few technicians.

Arguments such as these have been criticized in general on the essentially empirical ground that while some human behaviour may be accounted for in terms of forces which propel the actors, it is implausible that behaviour in general can be explained in this manner. Rather, there is a strong presumption that human behaviour is intentional, reflecting the observation that both waiting and indirect strategies are characteristic features of human choice (Elster 1979: 10, 116).

Some critics of the entrepreneurial-failure thesis do not fault it on explanatory grounds, but simply note that for each alleged instance of entrepreneurial failure it is possible to juxtapose examples of vigorous entrepreneurship (Kirby 1981: 9; Pollard 1989: 49–57; Saul 1967). If only certain firms or sectors were afflicted by the 'British disease', no generalized indictment of British entrepreneurship is justified:

The stronger form of criticism denies that cultural factors influenced the behaviour of British entrepreneurs. This brings us to the rational-choice approach to economic decline. According to this argument the behaviour of British businessmen may be understood in terms of rational actors optimizing intentionally subject to given constraints. Relative economic decline did take place, but the culprit was a particular set of constraints rather than any inept decision-making on the part of British entrepreneurs. One well-known neoclassical version of this argument, associated notably with the work of McCloskey (1981) on Victorian Britain, argues that markets were competitive and that the constraints were economic:[12]

The thesis expressed here is that the resources available to the economy were not elastic in supply and reallocation of them (capital abroad, for example) would have brought little or no additional growth. The growth of output depended on how productively the available resources were used. The measure of productivity suggests no great failure of Britain on this score ... The alternative is a picture of an economy not stagnating but growing as rapidly as permitted by the growth of its resources and the effective exploitation of the available technology (McCloskey 1981: 106).

The more common form of the neoclassical argument, particularly in the context of the debate on the post-World War II performance of the British economy and the policies of the Thatcher governments, identifies the constraints as institutional. The contention is that vested-interest groups, especially trade unions, have interfered with the efficient allocation of resources through the price system (Hayek 1986: 112–13):[13]

---

[12] Also see Floud (1981); Sandberg (1981).
[13] For journalistic accounts of this position, see Hoskyns (1986); Joseph (1986); *The Times*, editorial, 'The sparks are falling on the gunpowder' (13 Nov. 1979).

There can be no salvation for Britain until the special privileges granted
to the trade unions three-quarters of a century ago are revoked....
Britain can improve her position in the world market ... only by allowing the market to bring about a restructuring of her whole internal price
system. What is ossified in Britain is not the skill of her entrepreneurs or
workers, but the price structure and the indispensable discipline it im-
poses. The present British economic system no longer signals what has to
be done and no longer rewards those who do it or penalises those who
fail to do it.

The claim that trade unions in Britain have made almost everybody worse off by interfering with the price system can be criticized on both empirical and theoretical grounds. Elbaum (1989),
for example, has argued that the apprenticeship system established in British engineering through collective bargaining between the craft-unions and employers made a positive contribution to the sector's competitive performance during the late
nineteenth and early twentieth centuries. The strength of the
institution allowed apprentices to make credible commitments for
stability of employment even though their skills were transferable
among firms. This, combined with the low level of apprentice
earnings relative to their marginal products during the final years
of apprenticeship, encouraged employers to make initial investments in training by helping to assure that they would achieve a
return on their investment.

Freeman and Medoff (1984: chs. 10, 11) have made a similar
argument for the case of firm-specific skills. Companies that share
with their work-force the costs of investing in specific skills have
an interest in laying off workers according to seniority. Seniority-
based lay-off policies, by responding to workers' interest in job
security, serve to reduce labour turnover and increase the probability that the firm will secure a return on its initial investment.
Workers, however, may distrust management's promise to lay off
according to seniority, fearing that some unanticipated slump in
demand will lead management to adopt the lay-off policy that
maximizes the firm's chances of survival in the short term, for
example laying off the least productive workers. Fearing this,
workers will quit more frequently, reducing the firm's incentive
to invest in specific skills. They conclude that the presence
of a union, acting as an enforcer of commitments, makes

management's promises more credible and results in higher productivity.[14]

The general proposition, which both of these examples illustrate, has been developed by Arrow (1974: ch. 1). Organizations may be a means of achieving the benefits of collective action in situations in which the price system fails due to a failure of agents to optimize. A failure to optimize may transpire under conditions of uncertainty due to imperfect foresight because bounded-rationality considerations preclude fashioning complete contingent contracts that can be costlessly enforced by third parties (Nelson and Winter 1982: 35–6; Simon 1957: 39–41). These cognitive limitations give scope for opportunistic behaviour on the part of trading partners that can result in a breakdown of the relation and a failure to make mutually beneficial investments. (Arrow 1974: 35–6; Williamson 1985: ch. 2).

An example may help to illustrate the point. Suppose a worker is contemplating the negotiation of a contract with a firm which will allow him or her to break even on a proposed investment in firm-specific skills. Once the investment is made, however, the worker's vulnerability is increased since it will be impossible to move among firms without loss of productivity. The employer will be in a position to appropriate the worker's investment by demanding a downward renegotiation of the agreed wage, where the limit of this downward revision will be set by the difference between the original contract terms and the wage the worker can demand for entirely general skills in the external labour-market. The firm may justify the new contract terms in the name of unexpected financial difficulties which the worker in general will not be in a position to verify. Workers' concern that firms will behave in this opportunistic manner may discourage them from agreeing to invest in specific skills with the result that productivity is lower (Williamson 1985: ch. 10).

I want to raise one objection and one qualification to the market-failure argument. The objection is empirical. The claim that organizations can always be understood as means of achieving

---

[14] For a similar argument, see Williamson *et al.* (1975: 270) concerning the efficiency purposes of internal labour-markets established through collective bargaining with trade unions.

the benefits of collective action in situations in which the price
system fails is no more plausible than the assertion that atomistic
market competition is always the best guarantor of economic
well-being. Trade unions, for example, may serve the efficiency
purposes noted above, but they may also seek to raise the relative wages of their members which does not make everybody,
or almost everybody, better off. A more plausible position is
that trade unions serve multiple purposes, both monopoly and
efficiency ones.

The qualification concerns the agenda of organizations, or what
they do to achieve the benefits of collective action, and how their
agendas relate to the environment in which they operate. An
organization whose agenda is well suited to the state of the
environment at the time of its creation may prove less capable of
achieving its purposes when economic and technical conditions
change. In the British shipbuilding industry, for example, it is a
commonplace that the craft jurisdictions or demarcations around
which apprentice training was organized at the turn of the century, though well suited to the industry's requirements at that
time, proved to be less well adapted to the industry's needs
following the introduction of welding and prefabrication techniques during the 1930s and 1940s (see Ch. 5).

The idea that an organization may become rigid and retain the
structure acquired at its beginning raises the general issue of
whether institutions should be seen as binding constraints on the
behaviour of actors, or as being alterable and subject to their
intentional decision-making. The following discussion of the
institutional explanation for Britain's economic decline recently
developed by Elbaum and Lazonick (1986) illustrates the
importance of this distinction.

Elbaum and Lazonick's analysis draws substantially on
Chandler's (1977) work on the rise of the large corporation in the
United States during the twentieth century. They observe that
British firms with comparatively simple internal structures com-
peted successfully during the nineteenth century when they relied
extensively on the market to co-ordinate economic activity. Competitive success in twentieth-century manufacturing, however, requires sophisticated managerial hierarchies to assure control of
production standards and to co-ordinate the vertical integration

of production and distribution that is a prerequisite for effective utilization of mass-production techniques.[15] They explain decline by arguing that British businessmen, though rational, were constrained from adopting these modern corporate forms by institutional rigidities dating back to the nineteenth century. In a moment I shall argue that the retention of the rationality assumption results in an important inconsistency in their argument.[16]

In such countries as the United States, Germany and Japan, successful economic development in the twentieth century has been based on mass production methods and corporate forms of managerial co-ordination. Britain, however, was impeded from adopting these modern technological and organization innovations by the institutional legacy associated with atomistic, nineteenth-century economic organization. Entrenched institutional structures—in industrial relations, enterprise and market organization, education, finance, international trade, and state-enterprise relations—constrained the transformation of Britain's productive system (Elbaum and Lazonick 1986: 2).

The argument of Elbaum and Lazonick is incomplete for two related reasons: first, the failure to give a definition of institutions that specifies their relationship to human behaviour; and secondly, the failure to address in general terms why institutions should be unchanging or rigid.

A standard definition of an institution is a rule of behaviour that specifies action in particular recurrent situations (Hall 1986: 19; Langlois 1986: 247; Schotter 1981: 11). More loosely, an institution may be defined as 'the way we do things'. If we accept this definition, it is apparent that the argument that British businessmen, though rational acted in ways that resulted in relative economic decline because of the nature of British institutions,

---

[15] Elbaum and Lazonick do not develop the microfoundations for the position that mass production requires complex managerial hierarchies to co-ordinate vertically integrated-production processes and that the market is a comparatively poor mechanism for co-ordinating economic activity. For an attempt to provide these microfoundation, see Williamson (1985: chs. 4, 11).

[16] On the use of the rationality assumption, see Elbaum and Lazonick (1986: 2): 'As neoclassical economic historians have emphasized . . . British businessmen may in general have performed well by the test of cost minimization subject to prevailing constraints. Britain's problem, however, was that economic decision-makers, lacking individual or collective means to alter existing constraints, in effect took them as "given".' Also see Lazonick (1981: 37).

is not wholly consistent. It asserts that they behaved either conservatively or stupidly as the case might be, because that is the way they always did things; but how could this be if they were rational optimizers? Of course a different definition of institutions might satisfy this criticism, but, given the failure of Elbaum and Lazonick to provide such a definition, it is not apparent from their account what prevented British management from transforming institutional arrangements so as to compete more effectively.[17]

When the argument of Elbaum and Lazonick is scrutinized in this manner it becomes clear that their mode of explanation is actually the same as the neoclassical model they criticize. Rational agents are assumed to optimize, given their preferences, subject to pre-given institutional constraints. The question of whether institutions can be treated as pre-given constraints or should be seen as alterable, however, is one that needs to be handled with care and will depend on the case under consideration. If the institution or behavioural pattern is produced by the actors whose behaviour is being explained it is reasonable to argue that the institution should not be treated as a naturally given constraint, but rather as subject to their intentional decision-making. On the other hand, if the institution is produced by an agency external to the actors whose behaviour is being explained it may more plausibly be treated as a pre-given constraint.

For example, it has often been alleged that capital-market institutions resulted in sluggish growth in Britain prior to the First World War. In particular, the national banks are criticized for having refused to offer the long-term finance which firms required for investing in new large-scale methods at the turn of the century. The stock-market is thought to have provided a poor substitute for long-term bank finance (Kennedy 1976; Kennedy 1987; Saville 1961). While there is considerable debate over

---

[17] This general criticism is implicit in the comments of G. Saxonhouse and G. Wright on Lazonick's analysis of the cotton industry and the choice of British entrepreneurs between mule and ring spinning. Saxonhouse and Wright point out that while Lazonick argues that vertical specialization of production between spinning and weaving in Britain constrained the diffusion of ring spinning, there is no explanation offered for what 'blocked the path vertical integration' (Saxonhouse and Wright 1987: 87–9).

whether these features of British capital-market institutions constrained growth rates prior to 1914,[18] it is none the less plausible that individual firms took the policies of national banks and the inadequacies of the stock-market as given, and perceived themselves as constrained to rely on a combination of self-financing and the rolling over of short-term loans.

This line of argument is less plausible for such institutions as enterprise organization. In the case of the British shipbuilding industry, for example, it is unreasonable to argue that such institutional practices as the way labour and management organized production or conducted collective bargaining should be treated as naturally given constraints that also explain why these actors behaved in a manner that resulted in the industry's competitive decline. We require some explanation for the failure of management and labour to change the way they organized their affairs so as to improve the industry's chances of survival.

In the following chapters I present an institutional explanation for the British shipbuilding industry's competitive decline that avoids the pitfalls discussed above. In common with the work of Elbaum and Lazonick, I argue that the failure to transform institutional arrangements dating back to the nineteenth century is a key factor in explaining competitive decline. I do not examine all the institutions that have been earmarked as contributing to Britain's relative economic decline, but I focus on one key institution, enterprise organization, and on the system of labour management in particular.

Unlike the work of the institutional historians just discussed, I do not take as given the maintenance of the institutions in accounting for the behaviour of British businessmen during a period of declining competitiveness. Rather, I develop an intentional explanation for the failure of British businessmen to transform their constraints. The key assumptions and conditions of my argument are: *bounded rationality* or limitations in the ability of humans to process the mass of information required for making

---

[18] See Pollard (1989: ch. 2) for a critical review of the literature. Pollard concludes that in channelling a large part of national savings abroad the banks contributed to a deterioration of the British growth rate prior to 1914. In the case of the shipbuilding industry, however, Pollard and Robertson (1979: 82–4) find no evidence that the firms were capital-starved between 1870 and 1914.

the optimal decision; British management's *uncertainty* over the need for organizational change during the decade or so following World War II; and *lack of trust* between labour and management that resulted in a failure of co-operation over proposed institutional reform between 1958 and 1965.

My use of uncertainty is based on Arrow's (1984: 173) definition. The type of uncertainty to which I am referring here derives not from a lack of descriptions of states of the world which are complete for all relevant purposes, but from imperfect foresight that precludes assigning numerical probabilities to those states.

Uncertainty is also relevant in the context of strategic decision-making, but it derives from a different type of ignorance (Elster 1983: 12–15; Williamson 1985: 58). It is well known that in certain game-theoretic situations (notably the iterated Prisoner's Dilemma) there are multi-equilibria. Our uncertainty concerning the best choice of action in this context derives from bounded-rationality considerations. We lack complete information about the preferences and the beliefs of others and are also uncertain as to whether the knowledge we have about each other is 'common knowledge' (Binmore and Dasgupta 1986: 11, 21). Under these conditions, our choice of action will depend on our beliefs about others and in particular whether we believe them to be trustworthy.[19]

Lack of trust is the key to explaining the competitive decline of British shipbuilding. While I do not explore the origins of distrust between labour and management, I do stress its long legacy. Distrust in the shipbuilding industry dates back to at least the turn of the century, when conflict erupted over managerial efforts to exploit the possibilities offered by increased mechanization for substituting lower paid apprentices for fully skilled workers.

I would like to stress that my aim has not been to develop a general theory which applies to all institutions and their maintenance. Rather, I have set out to explain the maintenance of

---

[19] For the purposes of this book, 'trusting behaviour' means an action that (1) increases one's vulnerability to another whose behaviour is not under one's control, and (2) takes place in a situation where the penalty suffered if the trust is abused would lead one to regret the action. In short, there is no best strategy independent of trust. See Lorenz (1988 and 1991). For a general discussion of how trust can be brought about, see Gambetta (1988).

institutions in the British shipbuilding industry and their relation to competitive decline. Whether or not the explanation I have developed has wider applicability, remains to be seen.

III. Overview

The next two chapters describe the development of the shipbuilding industry's institutional structure from 1890 to 1939. Chapter 2 shows how product- and labour-markets in nineteenth-century Britain, together with the level of technology, fostered a highly fragmented industrial structure and a method of enterprise organization which I call the craft system. The craft system relied on the discretion and skills of the work-force for the co-ordination of the production process. Chapter 3 traces the development of trade-union organization and collective-bargaining institutions in the industry. It describes how the craft-unions, by bearing the costs of training and acting as labour exchanges in regional labour-markets, provided an institutional underpinning for the craft system. In both chapters I contrast conditions in British shipbuilding with those in the less successful French industry, where more bureaucratic[20] methods of enterprise organization were used, to point out the competitive advantage of Britain's comparatively informal system of work administration.

The fourth and fifth chapters investigate the causes of Britain's dramatic competitive decline after World War II. Chapter 4 shows how rapid growth in world demand for ships and increasing product standardization conferred the competitive advantage at this time on firms using more systematic planning methods. This progressively undermined the competitiveness of the craft system.

The first section of Chapter 5 argues that the failure of British

---

[20] Following A. L. Stinchcombe, I define 'bureaucratic' administration of work by the criterion that the following features of the work process are planned in advance by persons not on the work-crew: the location of tasks; the movement of tools, materials, and workers to these locations; sometimes the movements to be performed to complete tasks; the time allotments for tasks; and the inspection criteria for particular operations. In 'craft' administration of work, these characteristics of the work process are governed by workers in accordance with craft principles. See Stinchcombe (1959–60: 170).

shipbuilders to adopt more systematic planning methods during the decade or so following the Second World War can be explained in part by uncertainty. Their experience of severe demand fluctuations in the past made it rational for them to form cautious expectations about future market demand. British producers were concerned that the post-war boom would be followed by a collapse that would shift the competitive advantage back towards the non-bureaucratic system of work administration to which they were accustomed. The use of bureaucratic methods by competitors, however, did not reflect greater foresight on their part. Historically, shortages of skilled labour had constrained them to adopt top–down planning techniques. These shortages resulted in part from the lack of well-developed craft-unions or comparable institutions to assure the supply of skilled labour. All manufacturers, then, not just the British, continued to do what they always had done.

The second section of Chapter 5 develops the idea of enterprise organization as compromise in order to explain how the lack of trust between labour and management contributed to the failure to change. It examines a series of conflicts between 1930 and 1960 that were prompted by managerial proposals to alter established manning and payment arrangements to accommodate the introduction of welding and prefabrication technology. These employer initiatives were successfully resisted by the craft-unions who saw them as thinly veiled attempts to dilute the industry with lower paid and less skilled labour.

Chapter 6 presents a general analysis about economic decline and illustrates its relevance to the case of British shipbuilding. The argument in the first section of Chapter 5 suggested an evolutionary explanation, along the lines of Nelson and Winter (1982), in which firms fail or succeed according to their luck in meeting the right market conditions given their semi-randomly chosen strategies. The idea of the firm as compromise leads to a more elegant explanation. The failure to change should not be understood solely in terms of British management's 'blindness', much less their incompetence. While imperfect foresight meant the British shipbuilders were uncertain, during the decade or so following World War II, that changing market conditions would undermine the profitability of their established routines, they were certain, given the legacy of distrust, that any attempt to alter work-administration methods would lead to trouble with a work-force that would interpret any move as a trap. Under these conditions it was reasonable for British shipbuilders not to change.

British shipbuilders proposed comprehensive reform of methods of work administration after 1958 when industry profitability fell sharply. At this time, British management attempted to build up trust around proposed institutional reform. Reform only came about, however, following the closure of a number of the major yards between 1962 and 1965. Tragically, given the legacy of deep distrust, legitimizing the need for organizational reform amongst the work-force and their unions required visible pressures, such as firm bankruptcy or closure, that were perceived as originating from outside the organization. British businessmen may have been lucky when they succeeded, but they were not stupid when they failed, just constrained by lack of trust.

2

Shipbuilding—Industry Structure during the Craft Era, 1890–1939

MOST explanations for Britain's dominant position in world ship-building during the late nineteenth and early twentieth centuries emphasize the advantage British producers derived from the greater size of their market, which allowed for greater inter-yard specialization (Pollard 1957; Pollard and Robertson 1979: ch. 2; Parkinson 1960: 150–2). While my explanation for British competitive superiority similarly rests on the key role of market conditions, I argue that Britain was only able to realize the benefits of its advantageous economic position through the creation of a set of labour-market and enterprise institutions. These institutional arrangements, which I call the craft system, secured British producers adequate supplies of skilled shipyard labour with sufficient expertise to co-ordinate the work process independently of managerial supervision. Given the unstable market conditions in which shipbuilders operated, the non-bureaucratic British system of work administration proved competitively superior to the more bureaucratic methods typically used abroad.

This chapter describes the underlying economic and technical conditions which assured that competitive success in shipbuilding depended on employing a skilled work-force, sufficiently flexible to adapt to the unanticipated contingencies of the product market. Chapter 3 examines the institutional arrangements which secured British producers a work-force with these characteristics. I support the argument by means of comparing Britain's market conditions and institutional arrangements with those in the comparatively less successful French shipbuilding industry.

I. Market Structure

Probably the most thorough study of the basis for Britain's competitive success in shipbuilding prior to 1914 is that of Sidney Pollard (1957). Pollard has convincingly argued that the success of the British resulted from their having captured the expanding domestic market and much of the foreign market between 1860 and 1880. This was a period when competing maritime nations lacked developed iron, steel, and engineering industries and sufficient skilled labour to supply shipyards. Having captured these markets, British producers drew a critical advantage from the greater extent of the market they commanded, resulting in a greater continuity of demand for different classes of vessels. This allowed British builders to achieve a degree of specialization between yards that proved impossible in France or other maritime nations.[1]

A certain fraction of foreign demand was lost around the turn of the century, but the expanding domestic market continued to provide a secure source of demand for less expensive British vessels. As Table 2.1 indicates, the United Kingdom mercantile fleet increased by some 45 per cent between 1890 and 1910, while the United Kingdom percentage of the world fleet remained roughly constant.

The British shipbuilding industry was divided between two main districts and four rivers: the Clyde river in Scotland, and the Tyne, Tees, and Wear rivers on the north-east coast of England. There were about forty-five large builders on the Clyde between 1880 and 1900.[2] There were about fourteen firms on the Wear at this time, some fifteen to twenty on the Tyne, and eight or nine

---

[1] Pollard (1957: 433–6, 443–4); Pollard and Robertson (1979: 84–7). A number of French authors have developed the same argument, attributing higher French costs to the lack of continuity in demand for different types of vessels. See Basso (1910: 88–93); Hardy (1951: 39); Pinczon (1930: 96); Roux-Freissineng (1929: 31). Often the claims about the typical British producer were exaggerated: 'If you consider the English yard, you note, that given the extent of the market for ships, in this country, yards are able to put on the slip standard types of vessels, even in the absence of an order, in the certitude that the vessel will be rapidly purchased.' (Hardy 1951: 39.) In fact, production on a speculative basis was not typical in most British yards. See Reid (1980: 46).

[2] These figures exclude barge-, boat-, and yacht-builders.

TABLE 2.1. Net tonnage of the United Kingdom mercantile fleets, 1860–1910

Year	UK tonnage in 000s		UK %age of world total
	Sailing-ship	Steamship	
1870	4,577	1,112	33.94
1880	3,851	2,723	32.88
1890	2,936	5,042	35.50
1900	2,096	7,207	34.80
1910	1,113	10,442	33.37

Source: Kirkaldy (1919: app. xvii).

yards on the Tees, including the Hartlepools. Around the turn of the century the Clyde accounted for 30 to 35 per cent of mercantile tonnage produced nationally, while the north-east coast produced between 50 and 55 per cent in most years (Pollard and Robertson 1979: 62–3).

A certain amount of specialization took place on a regional basis. Yards on the Tyne and the Tees were highly specialized in cargo-vessel production, particularly unsophisticated cargo tramps. The Tyne was a mixed river, producing both sophisticated liners and naval vessels, as well as simple cargo ships. The Clyde, though known for its large passenger liners and warships, was the most diversified of the rivers, producing a range of vessel-types, including fishing, coastal, harbour, and cargo ships.

The remaining important shipbuilding districts were Belfast, Birkenhead, Barrow, and the east coast of Scotland. Barrow and Birkenhead specialized in warship production, while Belfast produced the largest liners. Fishing vessels were produced in Aberdeen, Dundee, and Leith on the Scottish east coast (Pollard 1957: 434).

While regional specialization may have resulted in certain economies due to concentration in one location of labour and suppliers who were suited to the demands of particular types of builders, yard specialization was more important in securing high productivity. Harland and Wolff; Clydebank; Workman, Clark and Co.; and Swan, Hunter and Wigham Richardson were the only yards which built giant express or 'intermediate' liners (Pollard 1957: 434). Vickers, John Brown, and Cammell Laird specialized in naval construction. In the smaller classes of vessels, I. P. Austin specialized in building steam-colliers, William Simon concentrated on dredges, and J. L. Thornycroft built fast warships and cross-channel ferries (Pollard and Robertson 1979: 85).

Specialization went furthest in the production of cargo tramps, where the dominance of British shipping interests was the greatest. Britain owned 90 per cent of the world's tramps prior to World War I. There were a variety of cargo design-types including the 'flush-decker', 'well-decker', and 'turret-decker' designs. Most of the early 'well-deckers' were built in the Hartlepools, and by 1889 some 350 such vessels had been built with an aggregate tonnage of over 500,000 (Silverwright 1888–9: 153; Holmes 1906: 102–30). Doxford and Sunderlands developed and specialized in the production of the turret-decker design, and by 1904 had constructed 100 of these vessels (Holmes 1906: 117).

Cargo tramps of the same design-type were not completely standardized, but were ships built to a similar pattern. Of the first fourteen 'turret-deckers' built by W. Doxford and Sons, two were 253 ft. in length, two were 280 ft., four were 297 ft., two were 340 ft., and the others were of varying dimensions. The tonnage of these vessels varied from 1,640 gross tons to 3,188 gross tons, and over the years the vessels increased in size and weight (Kendall 1894–5: 224). Individual angles, frames, plates, bulkheads, and stringers varied between ships of the same basic design-type but different lengths and tonnage.[3] Concentration on a design-type generated important increases in productivity, but it by no means meant standardization or mass production. There was little actual interchangeability of component parts in ship production, the closest approximation occurring in the production of sister ships; even in these cases different owners might make different scantling specifications.[4]

---

[3] See App. B for a glossary of technical terms.

[4] Pollard (1957) suggests that W. Doxford and Sons built 'turret deckers' by mass-production methods. There is no evidence, however, to show that mass-production methods, in the sense of using standard and interchangeable parts, were being employed. As I have pointed out, Doxford's built turret-decker tramps to vary dimensions.

The lack of product standardization significantly affected the shipbuilding industry's structure. It discouraged firms from expanding their scale of production, since even large yards were not in a position to benefit from the economies associated with series production of a standard product. Most firms retained labour-intensive production techniques that allowed them to readily adapt to unanticipated changes in product mix (Pollard and Robertson 1979: 28–9, 231).

There were offsetting influences in specialized segments of the market. The larger size and technical sophistication of liners and warships required the small group of firms specializing in their production to install larger berths, greater crane capacity, and a variety of specialized equipment for outfitting and ordinance work.

Liner specialists, in addition, were able to secure a degree of market protection through establishing close ties with owners. Large shipping lines such as the Cunard Line, the P. and O. Line, and the Furness Line had sufficient resources to build during recessions. This promised a stabilization of demand and encouraged a strategy of vertical integration between builders and owners, which, by lessening the risk of capital investment, encouraged these firms to expand the scale of their yards (Burn 1940: 272–4; Pollard and Robertson 1979: 92–6; Robertson 1975; Shield 1949: 55).

Warship builders acquired a similar degree of market protection from their established connections with the Admiralty, which restricted its contracts to a small and select list of yards whose equipment and methods of construction met strict standards. As the Admiralty tended to put greater emphasis on quality than on economy of construction, the few favoured firms did not face market constraints comparable with most commercial yards (Pollard and Robertson 1979: 211–14).

The large multi-yard establishment was the exception, however, during the early twentieth century. Table 2.2 provides evidence of the continued importance of small-scale production in British shipbuilding until 1930. During the boom that preceded and followed the First World War, industry output increased primarily through the creation of new firms, the large majority of which were single-yard establishments. During the subsequent contraction, there was only a marginal increase in average output per firm.

TABLE 2.2. Average output per yard and per firm in British mercantile shipbuilding, 1910–30

Year	No. of		Average output		Total output
	yards	firms	per yard	per firm	
1910	91	85	12.5	13.3	1,134
1920	126	109	16.3	18.9	2,056
1930	80	60	18.5	24.6	1,030

Note: These figures exclude boat-, barge-, and yacht-builders.

Source: The *Shipbuilder and Marine Engine Builder* (Jan. nos. of each year) for output per yard in British shipbuilding. Industry output figures from *Lloyd's Register of Shipping.*

During British shipbuilding's expansion throughout the period 1880–1914, the industry's fragmented structure did not prove an obstacle to securing the advantages of a comparatively high degree of specialization among the yards. The protracted recession of the inter-war period, however, resulted in a general scrambling for orders by British builders, and a breakdown of this specialization. The more technically versatile liner and naval specialists tended to encroach on the traditional markets of the commercial cargo producers. Beardmores, for example, a yard designed for naval construction, produced only one naval cruiser and two submarines during the eleven years prior to its closure in 1931. Armstrong-Whitworth, before its merger with Vickers in 1935, had diversified into commercial construction as well as loco- motive production (Jones 1957: 85–6, 134–5; Parkinson 1960: 30).

During the early 1930s persistent problems of excess capacity and the lack of inter-yard specialization motivated a nationally co-ordinated effort to restructure the shipbuilding industry.[5] This initiative resulted in a reduction in shipbuilding-industry capacity

---

[5] This restructuring took place in the context of the more general 'rationaliza- tion' movement which, to varying degrees, affected all Britain's staple industries. For a general discussion of the movement, see Hannah (1976). For an account of restructuring in the cotton textile industry, see Lazonick (1986). Tolliday (1987) presents a detailed account of restructuring in the steel industry during the 1930s. One of his principal conclusions is that a reorganization of financial control in the steel industry did not lead to a restructuring of the industry's technology or productive capacity.

but little change in the industry's technical organization or enterprise structure.

Restructuring during the 1930s

Rationalization in the shipbuilding industry was co-ordinated through the Shipbuilding Conference, which in 1929 entered into negotiations with the Bank of England to secure financial backing for the formation of the NSS.[6] The NSS was created for the specific purpose of purchasing redundant yards which were either to be dismantled or resold with restrictions on their future use for shipbuilding.[7] This was to be preliminary to a more basic restructuring of the industry through amalgamation into larger groups which was to provide a basis for greater inter-yard specialization by increasing the market power of individual firms (Bank of England, Central Archive, Accession no. 1/1020).[8]

While details of the negotiations required to set up the NSS are not available, it is clear that the co-operative arrangement was not the result of independent negotiations between the builders. Initially the scheme was not accepted by the majority of producers in the Sunderland district, who stayed outside the Shipbuilding Conference. Their eventual participation in the NSS depended on the backing of the Clearing Banks, who had acquired an important controlling interest in the industry through their overdraft facilities. A Bank of England memo for June 1929 noted that of the hundred yards to be included in the scheme, forty were in the 'hands of the banks' and thirty were in 'five hands'. A later memo reports Sir Lithgow enquiring of Montagu Norman how he might get in touch with the banks who 'control-

[6] The Shipbuilding Conference was established in 1928 with an initial membership of 27 to deal with commercial questions of general interest to mercantile builders. Eventually it came to include the large majority of the firms producing ocean-going tonnage. For a discussion of its price support activities during the inter-war years, see Slaven (1981).

[7] The Bank of England provided £2.5 million which was secured through a self-financing levy of 1% on all contracts of members of the Shipbuilding Conference. SRNA Archives, 'Statistics of the Shipbuilding, Shiprepairing, and Marine Engineering Industries, 1920–1939', sect. X.

[8] The deputation was composed of Sir J. Lithgow, who was chairman of Lithgows and the Ayrsdale Dockyard, and director of the Colville steel-works; and T. Thurlaway, chairman of Swan Hunter.

led' the industry in order to discuss the 'setting-up side of things' (Bank of England, Central Archive, Accession no. 1/1020).

The restructuring efforts of the NSS initially focused on the tramp-producing sector of the industry. Of the ninety-nine berths which had been purchased by the NSS by the end of 1932, eighty-seven were normally used for cargo-ship production. With the deepening of the crisis in 1933 and low order books in 1934 and 1935, capacity problems remained paramount, and a number of naval and liner specialists were closed: Swan, Hunter and Wigham Richardson's Southwick yard, Fairfields' West yard, and the three yards of Armstrong-Whitworth in 1935;[9] Workman, Clark and Co. in Belfast and D. W. Henderson on the Clyde (wholly owned by Harland and Wolff) in 1936 (SRNA Archives, 'Statistics of the Shipbuilding, Shiprepairing and Marine Engineering Industries, 1920–1939', sect. X).

The activities of the NSS were progressively wound down with the beginnings of recovery in 1936 and rearmament soon after. Only a further thirty-six berths were closed between 1937 and 1939. The Shipbuilding Conference estimated the industry's 1930 capacity at 3,900,000 tons. In total, through the activities of the NSS, 218 berths with an estimated capacity of 1,400,000 tons were closed, leaving a 1939 capacity of 2,500,000 tons, well over twice the level of output achieved during any single year in the 1930s. The NSS could scarcely have been considered a success by its own criterion.

Arguably more important in the long run than these capacity problems was the fact that amalgamation of the yards, which might have provided a basis for increased yard specialization, was not pursued in any systematic fashion. Certainly Lithgows acquired Fairfields in 1935. This, in conjunction with the 1919 purchase of W. Hamilton, transformed the firm into a large diversified producer, the two acquired yards concentrating on the production of liners and warships, while the parent yard produced tramps and increasingly tankers. The merger of Vickers with Armstrong-Whitworth also increased industrial concentration, but the sale of D. W. Henderson, and Caird and Co. (both

[9] The Walker yard, more oriented towards commercial building, was kept on a care and maintenance basis by Vickers-Armstrong.

TABLE 2.3. Industrial concentration in British mercantile shipbuilding

Year	% age of gross tonnage accounted for by			
	top 2 firms	top 3 firms	top 5 firms	top 10 firms
1920	19.1	27.4	34.4	45.5
1930	25.8	31.8	40.4	57.7
1938	24.5	34.0	46.4	65.8

Note: These figures exclude boat-, barge-, and yacht-builders.

Source: The *Shipbuilder and Marine Engine Builder* (Jan. nos. of each year) for output per yard in British shipbuilding. Industry output figures from *Lloyd's Register of Shipping*.

owned by Harland and Wolff) and the West yard of Barclay Curle (owned by Swan Hunter) worked in the opposite direction. As Table 2.3 shows, despite a large number of yard closures during the 1930s, there was only a marginal increase in industry concentration.[10]

As a result of the failure of these restructuring efforts, the British shipbuilding industry entered the Second World War with a structure little altered in its fundamental characteristics from that of the pre-1914 period. It remained composed of a large number of small- and medium-sized single-yard firms coupled with a few large multi-yard enterprises. The character of these firms as small producers operating in volatile markets affected in turn, as we shall see, their use of technology and their organiza-

[10] The number of yards per firm has been determined by a general reading of the literature: Pollard and Robertson (1979), Jones (1957), and Parkinson (1960). In 1938 the multi-yard firms were Lithgows with four yards; Harland and Wolff with two yards; Swan, Hunter and Wigham Richardson with four yards; Vickers-Armstrong with two yards; and Hawthorne Leslie with two yards. The yard output figures do not distinguish between warship production (measured in displacement tons) and mercantile output (measured in gross tons) and the concentration ratios for mercantile shipbuilding are somewhat upward-biased for this reason. In 1920 none of the firms figuring in the top ten commercial builders produced naval tonnage. The problem is slight in 1930, as only 20,000 displacement tons were launched by the private builders, and the only firm amongst the top ten producing warship tonnage was Swan, Hunter and Wigham Richardson. In 1938 the bias is somewhat greater, as 80,417 displacement tons were launched by private firms. Amongst the top ten firms, those ranked 1st, 2nd, 3rd, 7th, and 9th launched some naval tonnage.

TABLE 2.4. Net tonnage of the French mercantile fleets, 1860–1910

Year	French tonnage in 000s		French %age of world total
	Sailing-ship	Steamship	
1870	918	154	7.49
1880	641	277	6.39
1890	444	500	4.60
1900	501	528	3.93
1910	636	711	4.20

Source: Kirkaldy (1919: app. xvii).

tion of work, ensuring that a premium was placed on employing a highly skilled labour force.

A Comparison with France

The French industry provides a useful comparison for illustrating the advantages of Britain's large market. The comparatively small French domestic market grew at a slow rate relative to Britain's, as the French fleet declined from 6.4 per cent of world tonnage in 1870 to about 4 per cent at the turn of the century.

French builders relied on a series of protective laws starting with the 1881 law which provided bounties to builders to compensate for customs duties on imports of materials used, principally steel and coal. It also provided a subsidy to owners, but only at a half-rate for vessels purchased abroad. The legislation failed to shift the demand of French owners decisively toward French builders (Charpentier 1945: 183).

The 1893 law eliminated the half-subsidy to owners for vessels purchased abroad, while extending subsidization to sailing vessels. This resulted in an alarming increase in the production of obsolete steel vessels designed for sail-propulsion, from about 30 per cent of net additions to the fleet in 1893 to about 85 per cent in 1901. The 1902 law eliminated the worst excesses of this legislation by limiting the tonnage of sailing vessels to which the

TABLE 2.5. Location of French shipbuilders, 1900

Region	Firm[a]	Town
Channel	Établissement normand	Le Havre
	Chantiers de France	Dunkirk
	Anciens établissements Fatre	Rouen
	Chantiers de la Méditerranée	Graville
Loire-Inférieure	Établissement Dubigeon	Nantes
	Établissement Brosse et Fouche	Nantes
	Anciens établissements Fatre	Nantes
	Chantiers de la Loire	Nantes
	Chantiers de la Loire	Saint-Nazaire
	Chantiers de l'Atlantique	Saint-Nazaire
	Établissements et Chantiers nantais	Chantenay-sur-Loire
Mediterranean	Chantiers de la Méditerranée	La Seyne
	Chantiers des messageries maritimes	La Ciotat
	Chantiers de Provence	Port-de-Bouc
Other	Chantiers de la Gironde	Bordeaux

[a] Only yards capable of building vessels over 200 gross tons are included.
Source: Latty (1951: 250).

subsidies applied. This contributed to a sharp fall in total tonnage produced in France (Charpentier 1945: 183; Serot 1943: 83–4).

At the turn of the century the French industry was divided between three principal districts: the Loire-Inférieure (Nantes and Saint-Nazaire), the Channel (principally the Seine estuary), and the Mediterranean coast (principally Marseilles and La Ciotat). There were thirteen firms and fifteen yards as presented in Table 2.5 above.

The Loire-Inférieure was the largest of the districts at this time, accounting for over 50 per cent of national output around the turn of the century (see Table A.2). By 1914 the regional distribution of capacity had changed. An additional yard, Chantiers Dyle et Bacalan, had been opened at Bordeaux, and Chantiers de l'Atlantique had established a yard in Grand Quevilly on the site of abandoned yard of Chantiers Augustin Normand. The two yards of Établissement Fatre had been closed and Brosse et Fouche, following the acquisition of the Vorruz engine-works, had been reconstituted as the Ateliers et chantiers de Bretagne (Puech 1969: 151). At this time there were three major yards in Nantes: Chantiers Dubigeon, Chantiers de la Loire, and Chantiers de Bretagne. There were two in Saint-Nazaire: Chantiers de la Loire and Chantiers de l'Atlantique.

During World War I and the boom which followed, eight additional yards were established. Only four of these were still operating in 1930. These were: Worms et Cie at Le Trait, Chantiers navales français at Caen, Ateliers et chantiers maritimes du Sud-Ouest near Bordeaux, and Chantiers Delmas-Vieljeux at La Pallice (Puech 1969: 155).

The small size of the French market and the instability of demand limited yard specialization. With the exception of two warship builders producing for the Maritime nationale, Chantiers de la Gironde and the Établissement normand, none of the French builders were specialists. The more successful were closely tied to French shipping lines. Many, in fact, were created by shipping companies who were acting to secure their own source of supply. Chantiers Penhoët in Saint-Nazaire, for example, was set up by the Compagnie générale transatlantique in 1860, while the Messageries maritimes line opened a yard bearing its name at La Ciotat which operated from 1851 to 1916 (Barbance 1948: 365–6; Latty 1951: 761–4, 807–11).[11]

Later, after World War I, two shipping lines established their own yards: the Seine maritime yard by Worms et Cie; and the Delmas-Vieljeux yard by the Compagnie Delmas-Vieljeux in 1923. Chantiers de la Méditerranée was controlled jointly by four French liner companies: the Cyprien, Fabre, Chargeurs réunis, and Fraissinet lines. Chantiers de Provence was connected to the Fraissinet line and Chantiers de la Loire, though independent, built primarily for Chargeurs réunis (Latty 1951: 783–92, 803, 845).

Despite the advantages which commercial builders derived

---

[11] The Penhoët yard became independent in 1900, acquiring the name of Chantiers de l'Atlantique. The Messageries maritime yard was acquired by the Société provençale de construction navale in 1916. See Latty (1951: 761–4, 807–11).

from such connections, they were forced to produce a range of vessel-types in an effort to stabilize output. The Chantiers de l'Atlantique yard was typical in this respect. The yard was particularly suited for producing a large class of sophisticated vessel, especially transatlantic liners, and had produced such noted passenger liners as the *Rochambeau* (1911) and the *France* (1912). The yard also produced sophisticated naval cruisers and battleships such as the *Condorcet*. But, despite the suitability of the yard to this class of vessel, Chantiers de l'Atlantique also constructed tugboats, cargo vessels, torpedo-boats and fishing vessels (Barbance 1948: 390). Needless to say, in producing an occasional cargo ship, the yard could never approach the productivity of such British yards as W. Doxford and Sons which specialized in 'turret deckers'.

Suppliers to Shipbuilders

The economic benefits of a relatively large market and specialization in Britain extended to suppliers of steel and to manufacturers of ship components and fittings as well. Between 1910 and 1912 British shipyards consumed 30 per cent of national steel output and still accounted for 8 per cent in 1930. French yards were not only located at a distance from the principal steel districts in the North and East, but also purchased a comparatively small 0.5 per cent of national output in 1930. Their orders for steel plates and beams were special orders. This resulted in innumerable delivery delays and increased costs. There was no incentive for the French steel industry to produce standard runs of plates and angle-beams as the British producers could do profitably, given their comparatively assured market (Barbance 1948: 388; Pinzcon· 1930: 90; Pollard 1957: 438–9).

As the British market grew and the advantages of specialization were perceived, ship-component manufacturers specializing in the production of windlasses, pumps, interior fittings, and the like were encouraged to cater for the needs of particular builders, though the true potential for economies in this area was never realized (Pollard and Robertson 1979: 91; League of Nations 1927: 29). C. L. Le Maistre, representative of the BESA, complained in 1927 about the 'immense diversity of patterns leading to a lack of interchangeability and uniformity which handicaps the industry on all sides.... Different sizes and styles and patterns of quite ordinary pieces of apparatus, outside of proprietary articles, used on every class of ship, forces the manufacturer and distributor to carry large stocks, which turnover slowly because of this great diversity' (Le Maistre 1926–7: 805).

The shipbuilders to a large extent placed the onus for this state of affairs on the shipowners, claiming that they invariably insisted on individual scantling specifications. The opinion expressed was that owners were obstinate, and perhaps somewhat irrational in their idiosyncratic demands.[12]

The benefits of standardisation in some respects are obvious, but as a member of some of the Clyde panels, the feature that impressed me most was the diversity of opinion expressed by owners' representatives. In discussing such matters as derricks, bollards, etc., these gentlemen expressed absolutely opposite views. (Comments of J. L. Adam on 817 in discussion following C. L. Le Maistre's (1926–7) paper).

Le Maistre of the BESA was more hesitant to place exclusive blame, noting that standardization would require a gentlemen's agreement between owners and builders, such that all producers would be on the same basis when tendering. He disparaged what he saw as being a prevalent view, 'that standardisation interferes with invention and progress, and spells crystallisation' (Le Maistre 1926–7).

Thus, while the size of the industry led to the establishment of specialist ship-component producers, it is clear that the economic benefits derived were quite limited.

Lack of local coal and steel supplies for the major French builders located near Marseilles, in the Loire-Inférieure, and on the Seine estuary was a further handicap. The inability of the French coal industry to produce sufficient to meet home demand left French shipbuilding, as other sectors, dependent on imports, generally at higher prices than its rivals (Clapham 1968: 56–8,

---

[12] Also see J. L. Adam's comments on p. 816 in the discussion following Le Maistre's (1926–7) paper: 'The Shipbuilder is always standardizing his own work, whether he is aware of it or not; but the man that Mr. Le Maistre should get at is the shipowner . . . The shipowner knows exactly what he wants in order to carry out his particular work, and it is useless to endeavour to persuade him that because some other shipowner has something else, that will be good for him.'

234–5; Kemp 1971: 119). But it would be incorrect to over-emphasize the importance of this problem. State subsidization during the nineteenth century in France was designed to compensate for import duties and any price differential in materials. Furthermore, as Pollard has noted, two quite successful British yards, Harland and Wolff, and Workman, Clark and Co; both in Belfast, lacked local coal and steel supplies and had to bear the costs of sea-transport (Pollard 1957: 442). During the 1920s material costs in France were, overall, lower than in Britain, yet French builders still offered no effective competition (Dugas 1930: 60–2). Clearly, the causes of superior British performance lay elsewhere than in specialist component producers and proximity to and cheapness of raw-material supplies.

II. The Production Process

The analysis so far has attributed Britain's competitive edge in world shipbuilding to the greater extent of the British market and to the critical advantage of a higher degree of firm specialization. When considering the higher productivity of British labour at this time, a paradox arises (see Table 1.6).[13] It might plausibly be assumed that the greater continuity of demand faced by British producers would have encouraged them to invest in more up-to-date machinery and that the higher level of productivity was a result of greater mechanization. In fact, the situation was much the reverse. In so far as there were inter-country differentials in the degree of mechanization, British yards on average showed a preference for more labour-intensive methods.

Sidney Pollard has argued that the severity of cyclical fluctuations in shipbuilding output encouraged British producers to minimize capital expenditure in order to avoid the potentially crippling overhead costs that would be incurred during recessionary periods (Pollard and Robertson 1979: 28–9, 231).[14] The fact that most vessels were expensive custom-made commodities,

---

[13] For additional evidence of comparatively high labour productivity in Britain, see Basso (1910: 89) and Chasseriau (1901: 246).

[14] See Fig. 4.1 for fluctuations in world shipbuilding output between 1890 and 1939.

built with the close consultation of the owner who usually would pay in instalments while the vessel was being constructed, meant that a strategy of speculative construction and stockpiling of a standard commodity was not feasible (Reid 1980: 46–7). All shipyards necessarily faced periodiç depressions in demand and output. This encouraged British builders to preserve labour-intensive methods and to lay off labour during cyclical down-swings (Pollard and Robertson 1979: 29, 42; Reid 1980: 47).

American producers, on the contrary, lacking adequate sup-plies of labour and in response to the higher price of labour fitted out their yards around the turn of the century with expensive cranes and mechanical haulage equipment that only proved pro-fitable during periods of peak demand and led to bankruptcy in certain cases. While wages were lower in Germany during the nineteenth century, firms, similarly opted for more capital-intensive methods than in Britain, apparently in response to having inadequate pools of labour from which to draw. However, Pollard argues, the greater mechanization of foreign yards could not compensate for the superiority of British labour (Pollard and Robertson 1979: 40; Pollard 1957: 437; Royal Commission on Depression in Trade 1886, 3rd Report: 186–95, evidence of J. Scott).

While Pollard's analysis is illuminating in many respects, parti-cularly in developing a connection between the shipbuilding busi-ness cycle and technical choice, I would argue that it needs to be qualified in certain important respects. First, if higher labour productivity in Britain cannot be attributed to greater mechaniza-tion, then its basis in such factors as superior training or greater motivation remains unexplored. Secondly, in the particular case of France, yard equipment does not appear to have been substan-tially different from that in Britain during the late nineteenth century, though a clear superiority is documented for the inter-war years (Bartin 1884: 132–3; Royal Commission on Depression in Trade 1886, 3rd Report: 192, evidence of J. Scott; Dugas 1930: 58–9; Pinczon 1930: 89–90). Finally, and most importantly, I would argue that it is incorrect to describe the difference between British and German or American yards as the result of a general strategy of substituting capital for labour. Due to the customized nature of ship production and its consequent complexities, it was usually impossible to eliminate skilled labour from the production process. Rather, American and German builders substituted machinery for less skilled labour, particularly in mechanizing their cranes and haulage equipment. It was in this area that differences in the degree of mechanization were most pronounced and in which British admiration for the boldness of foreign design was evident (Fairburn 1902: 266): 'they had built all their berths exactly the same breadth, so that they could take this enormous crane (100 tons), run it up to the end of the slip, put it on to the transportation carriage, run it along the upper ends of the slips and put it on to any one of them in a very short time.' Certain of the larger British yards adopted similar methods before World War I. Harland and Wolff in Belfast built a gantry with hydraulic equipment, and Swan, Hunter and Wigham Richardson at Wallsend was equipped with a covered berth and electrical cranes. The majority, however, retained their fixed cranes, manually operated derricks, and push-carts on rails (Hume 1976: 167–8).[15]

While British producers were also slower in adopting more advanced systems of drive — substituting electric for steam-driven machines — and tended to retain the system of belt drive from a line-shaft longer than competitors, this had little bearing on actual skills (Craig 1917–18: 285; Pollard 1957: 436; Hume 1976: 169–70; Wallace 1894–5). The major exception to this general trend was that of pneumatically powered riveting machines which did decrease the required skill for riveting and which were extensively introduced in France and other countries prior to 1914, but not in Britain until the war-years (Barbance 1948: 386; Board of Trade 1932: 39–40). However, the restrictions that the Boilermakers' Society successfully placed on the use of the machines, ensured that they were operated by a full squad of three skilled men despite the need for only two and despite their suitability, as some employers argued, for use by semi-skilled labour.[16]

With the idea in mind, then, that the development of ship-

[15] Manually operated equipment was typical in Britain during the inter-war years as well. See Dugas (1930: 58–9).

[16] For a description of the conflicts surrounding the introduction of pneumatic machinery at the turn of the century, see Ch. 3.

building technology was uneven in nature and partial in its impact, it would seem useful to explore its development in some greater detail, considering in particular the impact of mechanization on skill requirements. For, if it is wrong to argue that foreign producers were somehow able to mechanize and eliminate their need for skilled labour while only Britain relied on its labour force, it would be equally wrong to argue that shipbuilding work was largely artisanal in character, and that hull-construction machinery remained unchanged, either in Britain or abroad, from its origins in the British tinsmithy and boilershop practices of the 1840s and 1850s (the *Engineer*, 5 May 1889; Hume 1976).

Technical Change and Skills

The shipbuilding production process began with the preparation of the draught plan, a set of small-scale designs showing the lines or body-plan of the vessel, and on the basis of which steel plates and other sections were ordered. These small-scale designs were then transformed into more detailed full-scale drawings in the mould-loft and faired or corrected for dimensional accuracy. On the basis of these, various wooden templates and models were constructed to assist the metal-working trades, including the scrive-board, a large section of wooden flooring into which the lines or body-plan of the vessel were cut to full scale (Reid 1980: 83).

Following this initial design and technical stage of production, the basic operations in shipbuilding were to punch and drill holes in plates and angle-iron bars, to cut and shape the components, and to rivet the pieces together at the berth. Work generally began with the preparation of the angle-bars which formed the frames or ribs of the vessel. The first job was to mark the positioning of the rivet-holes on the flange of the bars to which the plates would eventually be joined. Marking was done on the basis of the scrive-board. A long flexible batten was bent to the shape of the appropriate line on the scrive-board and the positioning of the rivet-holes marked. These specifications were then transferred to the angle-bar which was punched, either with a combination punching and shearing machine, which was primarily designed for plate preparation, or with a specialized angle-cutting machine, generally with horizontal action (Holms 1918: 548–50; Hume 1976: 161–2).

The marking and punching of frame angles, though apparently a straightforward task, required a considerable amount of experience. When the angle-frames were bent to the appropriate curvature after punching, the flange or flat collar would naturally stretch at the bilge (rounded portion of the hull between side and bottom) and consequently in the initial marking of the landings showing the positioning of rivet-holes, necessary adjustments had to be made from what was actually specified in the scrive-board to prevent the holes from being too far apart after bending. In marking the frames, the workman would slip the landings down an inch or two so that the holes were marked closer than actually desired. And the amount was something that was learnt from constant experience (Holms 1918: 474).

After marking and punching, the highly skilled task of frame-bending would commence. Bending was done on a cast-iron floor composed of slabs or blocks, from five to six square foot, and pierced with holes for holding pins. The bending process consisted of fixing a flat bar of soft iron called a 'set iron' to the appropriate frame scrive, marking the position of the top of the frame and the bevel lines and fixing it to the bending blocks by means of pins. While the set was being fixed, the frame angle was heated and when sufficiently furnaced was bent by the helpers under the direction of a smith to the shape of the set using levers and iron bars to force the bar to the appropriate shape and 'dogs' or pins to fix its position (Holms 1918: 475–6; Abell 1948: 132–3). The appropriate bevel was then given to the bar, either manually by a bevelling lever applied to the angle's flange or by machine tool. The bending process required a high degree of skill. Not only did bars have to be furnaced to the correct degree, but on cooling, the frame bars would tend to straighten slightly. The angle-smith had to compensate for this by increasing slightly the bend of the set beyond that indicated on the scrive-board (Holms 1918: 476; Reid 1980: 107).

Plate preparation was done on the basis of full-scale wooden templates. These were either produced in advance in the mould-loft on the basis of the full-scale drawings, or alternatively the workman could 'lift' the necessary information directly from the partially constructed frame of the vessel. Regardless of the procedure used, after marking, the plates would be punched and sheared using a crane to hoist them into the gap or gullet of the combination punching and shearing machine, one of the basic shipyard machine tools. The lightest of these were hand-operated, while the heavier machines designed for the thicker sections operated on steam-power transmitted by belt drive from a line-shaft (Hume 1976: 169). Plates were then machine-planed, a relatively simple operation, and countersunk prior to being given the appropriate curvature.

Originally most plate-straightening and plate-bending was done by hand after sections were heated in a furnace. With the switch from iron to steel in the 1880s in Britain, allowing for easier manipulation of plates in the cold state, powerful hydraulic bending rolls were generally adopted which did decrease the amount of skill and expertise required as compared with earlier hand methods (Reid 1980: 113–18).

Despite this partial mechanization process, plate preparation continued to require considerable precision and experience. Small mistakes in marking could result in 'unfair' holes and poor alignment of plates, requiring additional work for correction. Plate-bending could be difficult when both transverse and longitudinal bend had to be given to the same plate. In such a case, the plate would be given an excess of transverse curvature, some of which was lost when the longitudinal curve was given (Reid 1980: 112).

Punching and shearing machines were similarly on hydraulic drive and produced in increasingly large dimensions as plate size and thickness increased with the switch to steel. As J. R. Hume (1976: 160) explained:

Because rivet holes were normally the same diameter as the thickness of the plate, and since the power required and hence the strength of the machine frame increased as the cube of the diameter, an apparently modest increase in thickness of plate could have a marked effect on machine size. In 1881 a 1½ by 1½ in. punching and shearing machine weighed 21½ tons as compared with 14½ tons for a 1¼ by 1¼ in. machine of similar construction.

Thus, by the end of the nineteenth century, the use of the furnace was only required for frame-bending, though here, as the size of angle-bars increased, hydraulic rams or 'bears' were introduced to assist in the bending process (Hume 1976: 163; Holms 1918: 475–6).

The erection of the frames began with the laying of the keel. This involved first the laying of keel-blocks, which were simply cuttings from pine logs. Metal keel-bars were then laid on the blocks, faired, and held erect by ferrings nailed on the blocks and by transverse shores or wooden props which supported the frames. The actual erection of the frames began with the riveting together of three component parts which formed a unit, a frame angle, reverse bar, and floor plate, this generally being done at the berth. These units, starting at midships, were then lifted in place, either by upright derricks or a travelling gantry, and temporarily held in place by wooden battens. Other structural members, running both in the fore and aft direction and athwart ships, were then filled in until the framework was bound as one piece (Abell 1948: 134–5; Holms 1918).

When a number of frames were erected the structure would be faired to assure proper alignment of the 'shell landings' or lines marked on the frames to indicate the positioning of plates. With this under way, the process of riveting the shell plates to the frames and caulking the overlapping-plate seams began.

The ship's plating was constructed of overlapping strakes or rows of plates and the riveting procedure was to begin with the garboard or lowest strake, an inside one, to follow with successive inside strakes, and then to add the outside rows. First, the surfaces to be joined were brought into close contact by screwing up every third or fourth hole with screws and bolts. The rivets would then be heated and inserted into the holes and held in place with a holding-up hammer, while the protruding end was hammered to form a flush surface. The overlapping seams of the shell plates were then caulked or closed watertight. The procedure was to make a groove down the edge of the overlapping plate, setting a burred edge in contact with the inside plate. The split part was then forced into contact with the surface below (Abell 1948: 137; Holms 1918: 316).

Since riveting and caulking were essentially repeat work, requiring a great deal of exertion but little variation in actual physical motion, they were eminently susceptible to mechanization. Mechanical steam-riveters were apparently in general use for boilermaking in the 1870s, but being cumbersome and heavy were little used in shipbuilding. A hydraulic riveter was invented by R. H. Tweddell in 1883, but it was also adopted slowly due to its great weight (over half a ton) and lack of manœuvrability (Hume 1976: 165; Holms 1918: 309).

The use of hydraulic riveters was largely confined to connecting components which could be brought to the machine, such as frames, reverse bars and floors, or component parts of built beams (Holms 1918: 309). Harland and Wolff, which specialized in the largest class of vessels, was exceptional in having developed by the late 1890s an elaborate travelling gantry which could suspend and move the machine along the hull's surface (Holms 1918: 309).

A potential solution to the problem of mechanizing riveting and caulking came with the introduction of pneumatic machine tools at the turn of the century. These machines were relatively light and could be handled by one man and had the advantage over hand-work of being easily operated in confined spaces. Prior to World War I though, the full potential for labour-saving mechanization implicit in these machines was never realized in Britain, due to the careful controls which the Boilermakers' Society placed over their use (Reid 1980: 135–6).

Shipyard machine tools, then, evolved from rather simple beginnings in boilershop practice to an increasingly specialized and heavy class of machine tool designed to manipulate large and extremely heavy steel sections. While these machine tools were specialized to the methods of shipbuilding, they were by no means single-purpose tools, designed for the mass production of identical components. This point cannot be stressed enough. The absence of standardization in ship production assured that shipyard machine tools as they developed were not semi-automatic or single-purpose, capable of being used to produce similar or identical components in mass with a minimum of skill. These machines rather had to remain sufficiently versatile to be used to punch, shear, bend, etc., a variety of components of differing dimensions. Correspondingly, many of the operations performed with these machines required a skilled hand, as considerable precision and care was needed in marking and positioning the components while they were being processed. Indeed, most machine tools were not necessarily introduced with the intent of deskilling craft-workers, but with the intent of enhancing the productivity of skilled workers.

Similar considerations apply to much of the outfitting work that was done by sheet-metal-workers, iron- and brass-moulders, plumbers, joiners, and electricians. For, even in cases where outfitting components came to be produced outside the yards in standard runs by methods suitable for less skilled workers, the assembly and fitting of these components into a non-standard ship continued to require skill (Reid 1980: ch. 6).

Plumbers and coppersmiths, for example, made increasing use of standard factory-produced pipe fabrications after the 1870s. In order to fit these into the vessel, it was necessary to read plans, take sets (templates), and to shape the finished piping. The heating and bending of the pipes required considerable care and expertise to avoid buckling or undue stress which would result in a loss of strength (Ministry of Labour 1927–8: 53). The ever-changing scantling specifications of successive vessels assured that the job remained a non-repetitive one, with little scope for using sets repeatedly. It continued to require a skilled hand and sound judgement based on experience.

These remarks apply equally to fitting electrical components and to the work of joiners who produced such items as wooden furniture and wall-cabinets. Indeed, as A. Reid (1980: 185–6) has pointed out, the introduction of machine tools such as the circular saw, planing and edge-preparation machine, and sand-papering machine tended to increase rather than decrease skill requirements, as employers took advantage of the machines' capabilities to produce more complex shapes.[17]

Thus, prior to the late 1930s and the 1940s when the general application of arc-welding and gas-burning technology contributed to a period of radical change in shipbuilding methods, mechanization in the sense of using labour-displacing machines

---

[17] For descriptions of the skilled nature of the work of sheet-metal-workers, tinsmiths, and iron- and brass-moulders, see Ministry of Labour (1927–8: 51–3).

was largely confined to the more routinized and less skilled tasks of moving components and equipment around the yard, and to riveting components together. These stringent limitations on the use of labour-displacing machinery in shipbuilding in turn meant that competitive success depended on having a skilled and versatile work-force. In the following chapter I will examine the distinct constellation of political forces and institutions which, in this regard, placed British builders in an internationally superior position.

3

Shipbuilding Employment Relations during the Craft Era, 1890–1939

In the previous chapter I argued that the distinct market conditions under which shipbuilders operated during the late nineteenth and early twentieth centuries guaranteed that a premium was placed on employing a highly skilled work-force. In this chapter I investigate the economic and institutional factors which assured British builders adequate supplies of skilled labour. I continue to make use of a comparison with conditions in the less competitive French shipbuilding industry in order to highlight the factors accounting for Britain's success.

The discussion begins by showing that broad political differences between the countries favoured British industrialists in terms of the potential supply of labour. I then turn to differences in industrial structure and institutional arrangements at the local level that help explain the comparative success of the British in maintaining pools of skilled labour in the principal shipbuilding districts. I argue that periodic shortages of skilled labour in French shipbuilding resulted in a distinctive pattern of shipyard employment relations, as well as a tendency to adopt more bureaucratic methods of work administration designed to economize on the use of skilled manual labour.

I. National Patterns of Labour Supply

Comparative histories of nineteenth-century industrial development in Britain and France have traditionally taken France's relative backwardness as the point of departure. Recent revisionist accounts have contested this perspective. First, based on revised estimates of per capita commodity production and labour productivity, it has been argued that the performance of the French economy was comparable with that of the British (O'Brien and Keyder 1978: ch. 6). Secondly, it has been argued that British and French industrial development took place in distinct ways involving specialization in the production of different types of products to which techniques of production and enterprise organization were adapted. In short, France was not the tardy emulator of Britain, but rather pursued a different path of development (Levy-Leboyer 1968; O'Brien and Keyder 1978; Roehl 1976; Sabel and Zeitlin 1985).

While the productivity estimates which form the basis for the revisionist claim of comparable French performance are based on questionable assumptions, the proposition that France pursued a distinct pattern of development rests on more sure footing.[1] Patrick O'Brien and Calgar Keyder, who have argued the revisionist case most systematically, interpret the difference between the British and French pattern of industrial development as follows. In Britain, the existence of large and expanding markets at home and abroad for relatively undifferentiated products encouraged an early transition to the mechanized factory system of production. In France, the slower growth and geographical segmentation of the domestic market and the smaller proportion of output produced for export encouraged the retention of smaller scale artisanal forms of production. Small-scale skill-intensive methods were particularly suitable for satisfying locally differentiated demands (O'Brien and Keyder 1978: 160–74; Heywood 1976; Johnson 1979).

This stark comparison of British and French economic development overlooks the considerable diversity within each economy. As J. H. Clapham (1968: ch. 5) and more recently R. Samuel

---

[1] The case for comparable French performance has been made most forcefully by O'Brien and Keyder (1978). Their empirical results have been questioned by Crafts (1984). Crafts argues that O'Brien and Keyder's use of commodity production (excluding the service sector) for a comparison of economic performance is misleading and that in terms of gross national product (including services) British performance was superior. Crafts concludes, however, that the performance of the French economy during the 19th-cent. was considerably more respectable than suggested by earlier accounts stressing France's 'retardation'. See e.g. Kindleberger (1964) and Kemp (1971).

(1977) have stressed, small-scale labour-intensive methods retained considerable importance in Britain throughout the nineteenth century. On the other hand, the factory system did make
inroads on the workshop sector in France, particularly from the
mid-nineteenth century onwards (Gille 1959; Levy-Leboyer
1968). The basic contrast, however, is not in dispute. The French
1906 industrial census presents a striking picture of the vitality of
small-scale forms of production. Establishments with less than
ten employees accounted for 56 per cent of the industrial work-
force (Levy-Leboyer 1976: 98).

Regionally differentiated patterns of product-market demand
in France can be explained by the persistence of rural society and
the relatively slow pace of urbanization. This in turn can be
linked to the slow growth of population and the ability of the
land to absorb additional supplies of labour throughout
the nineteenth century, which limited the flow of population into
the cities (Lequin 1978). The agricultural sector in France
absorbed some 2.5 million additional inhabitants during the
nineteenth century and as late as 1914 agriculture accounted for
about 60 per cent of the labour force engaged in commodity
production. In Britain, the agriculturally employed labour force
expanded slowly during the first half of the nineteenth century,
reaching a peak of 2 million between 1845 and 1854. There was
a subsequent decline to 1.6 million in the period 1895–1904.
During this same period the industrially employed work-force
expanded dramatically, from some 1.6 million in the period
1803–12 to 7.4 million in the period 1895–1904. By 1914 industry
accounted for over 80 per cent of the labour force engaged in
commodity production (O'Brien and Keyder 1978: 94).

While an explanation of the differential rates at which agriculture and industry absorbed labour in Britain and France is
beyond the scope of this discussion, it is important to recognize
the political dimensions of the process. Most accounts, though
accepting that geographical conditions played a role, emphasize
the importance of differences in property rights and, in particular, the greater success of the French peasantry in defending their
rights to land (Labrousse 1966; Le Roy Ladurie 1970; Sargent
1961). The origins of this difference are obscure, and arguably
date back to the Middle Ages and the efforts of the monarchy in

France to prevent the seigneurs from encroaching on its tax base by reinforcing the peasantry's prerogatives. Comparable efforts by the crown in Britain were ineffectual and, in general, parliament and king facilitated the process of enclosure (Bloch 1952 and 1967; O'Brien and Keyder 1978: 132–5).

The viability of the small agricultural proprietorship in France during the nineteenth and early twentieth centuries contributed to labour-supply problems for large industrial employers. The availability of this option in combination with slow population growth limited the ability of industrial employers to recruit and retain a large number of workers. The problem was not merely the slow growth of potential supply, but also one of the preferences which small proprietors in agriculture repeatedly showed themselves capable of defending through political action.[2] Thus, differences in the wider balance of power between economic interests in each country and in their relation to the state or political centre contributed to structuring the supply of labour in particular ways.

II. Employment Policies

Shortages of labour with the requisite skills were a source of intermittent complaint in France from the earliest years of iron and steel ship-construction. A French naval engineer, L. E. Bartin, made the following remarks based on his 1884 investigatory mission to Britain (Bartin 1884):

Our general installations, our different manner of working ... and our equipment are relatively rich; what we do not possess to the same degree perhaps is a work-force raised at the doors of the workshops, seeing work in iron since their youth, instructed by tradition, trained by competition ...

In the period 1909–10 a group of Clyde engineers, who had been called in to oversee the construction of two large passenger liners

---

[2] Marx's characterization of French attitudes at mid-19th-cent. are much to the point. 'The position of a proprietor, the possession of a house, of a plot of ground, is the chief object also of the factory operative, and also of almost every poor man who has not already a property; in fact all look to the land.' (Marx 1976: app., 1075–6.)

at the Chantiers de l'Atlantique in Saint-Nazaire, expressed sur-
prise that the French did not follow the British practice of an
initial rapid erection of the frames on the berth, but, rather
proceeded in a more piecemeal fashion. The French had adopted
this method due to a lack of skilled labour and a need to economize on its use (Barbance 1948: 388).

In a similar vein, during the 1929–30 boom Dugas noted the
difficulties French builders were encountering in recruiting a
stable force of skilled workers (Dugas 1930: 59):

Unemployment is practically non-existent. The shipyards do not have
any flexibility from the point of view of labour power. They are not able
to recruit personnel with a view to a solid increase in production, and are
obliged, during the periods where they have few orders, to retain workers who they are not able to fully employ due to the risk of losing them
permanently.

One response of industrialists generally in France to problems
of labour supply was the adoption of paternalistic policies. In
such diverse sectors as textiles, machine-building, steel, and
paper it is easy to find examples of large employers providing a
range of social services, including low-cost housing and medical
services, designed to attach their workers to the factory by creat-
ing a sense of company loyalty (Levy-Leboyer 1976: 94–5;
Stearns 1978: 42–8).

In the case of shipbuilding industry during the late nineteenth
and early twentieth centuries, such strategies proved impractical
due to the industry's particular technical and market conditions.
Ships, as we have seen, were large and complex products built in
a series of stages requiring different skills. The large variation in
the skills required for different stages meant that the only way
employers could hope to stabilize their demand for specialized
workers was to plan carefully the sequence in which successive
vessels were produced. This would allow specialized trades to be
transferred from one ship to the next without being periodically
laid off. However, market constraints generally precluded this
sort of scheduling.

In both Britain and France between 1890 and 1940 most construction contracts were bespoke, vessels being built on demand
to the precise specifications of the owner. Further, builders faced

sharp fluctuations in the overall level of demand for new construction. These highly unpredictable market conditions discouraged a policy of speculative construction that would have allowed
producers to anticipate and plan a yard's future labour requirements (Basso 1910: 88–93; Hardy 1951: 34; Pollard and
Robertson 1979: 6–7, 28–30, 231–2). Given the high cost of
an individual ship relative to the total value of a yard's annual
production, failure to sell a single vessel which had been
produced on a speculative basis might well prove financially
crippling.

The contrasting employment policies which British and French
builders pursued in response to this general problem were partly
determined by differences in the size and structure of the industry
in each country. The British industry, as we have seen, was
highly fragmented, being divided between two districts each composed of forty to forty-five firms, the large majority of which
were single-yard establishments. As each producer's relative demand for particular types of skills varied over time, he would hire
and lay off workers with specialized skills who continuously
moved between the numerous yards in the industrial district
(Price 1981: 6–8, 12). In this manner, pools of skilled labour
were built up and maintained in the industrial districts during the
nineteenth century, and the division of labour was extended,
resulting in greater specialization of the work-force. Thus, the
original iron-workers of the 1830s and 1840s developed into
platers, angle-iron smiths, caulkers, riveters, holders-up, and
their assistants. A similar process subdivided engineering workers
into fitters, turners, and drillers. With the increasing specialization and sophistication of vessels, plumbers, electricians, brass-
moulders, coppersmiths, and other specialized outfitters were
brought into the industry.

Specialization was even extended to establishing a detailed
division of labour within individual trades, being most highly
developed in the case of the plating and angle-iron-smithy
squads. These squads worked on the basis of a modification of
the internal contract system, being paid so much per row of
plates or per set of frames, and being responsible for organizing
their semi-skilled assistants who were paid on a time-basis. Within the plating squads, the skilled men divided up the work, one

man to templating and marking, two to rivet-hole punching and shearing, two to bending plates, one man to furnacing plates of awkward shape, and one to positioning plates at the berth (Holms 1918: 527). Furthermore, platers tended to specialize in either light or heavy work (Reid 1980: 111). Angle-iron smiths adopted a similar detailed division of labour.[3]

French builders were unable to extend the division of labour to the same extent as their British counterparts. This can be explained in part by the comparatively few yards in any one district which meant that French builders as a group were not able to achieve the same continuity in demand for workers with specialized skills. Further, given the pervasive problem of skilled-labour scarcity, builders were reluctant to pursue a 'hire and fire' policy as in Britain, fearing a permanent loss of trained labour. Responding to these constraints, French builders tended to employ their skilled workers in a less specialized manner. In this way they attempted to avoid the necessity of laying off workers with every change in demand for specialized skills (Dugas 1930: 59):

> In France production is much more irregular and less homogeneous. The same worker is called upon to work successively on a naval vessel, on a cargo vessel, and in this on the most diverse parts of the same vessel. Whatever might be his professional worth, his productivity cannot be the same as if he was truly specialized.

The more flexible use of skilled labour in French yards responded to the problem of non-cyclical-based instability in de-

---

[3] Holms (1918: 473). While increasing specialization of the work-force in the British shipbuilding industry from the mid-19th-cent. onwards acted to narrow the range of tasks an individual worker was called upon to perform, and so decreased skill requirements, it is important not to confuse this specialization with the more extreme forms of the division of labour associated e.g. with Adam Smith's example of pin manufacture. The complexity of the product and its customization meant that it was not possible to specialize labour to the extent where a worker repeatedly performed one simple task at one location in the flow of production. The division of labour in shipbuilding rather had a broader occupational or craft basis. Even in the case of the plating squads, where the division of labour was pushed the farthest, it should be appreciated that this internal division of labour was established autonomously by the squad with a view to improving piece earnings, and it was only the working knowledge that each of the squad members had of the requirements for plating as a whole that allowed them to co-ordinate their work in relation to that of their squad partners.

mand for specialized skills, but not to the problem of instability in overall demand for labour. The shipbuilding industry experienced severe and protracted depressions between 1890 and 1939.[4] Laying off workers during cyclical down-swings potentially posed the problem of loss of labour with shipyard skills to competing sectors, which possibly offered more stable employment prospects (AREMORS 1983: 16–17).

British builders were clearly less concerned by this problem than their French counterparts. There is little evidence to suggest that British producers were constrained by labour-supply bottlenecks. This can be explained by the well-developed system of craft-unionism which secured British shipbuilders adequate supplies of skilled labour.

III. Trade-Unionism and the Craft System

By the end of the nineteenth century a high degree of union organization had been achieved by the skilled trades in British shipbuilding. Seventeen unions organized the majority of the skilled workers and the closed shop prevailed in the major yards.[5]

There were two principal unions organizing preparatory staff. Mould-loft personnel, who produced wooden templates to assist the metal-working trades, were organized by the SSA. The SSA was formed in 1881 through a reorganization of the United Kingdom Amalgamation of Shipwrights, a loose federation of local shipwright societies (Dougan 1975: 116–17). Patternmakers, who were responsible for producing three-dimensional wooden models, mostly for use by brass- and iron-moulders, were organized by the United Patternmakers Society (Reid 1980: 88).

The United Society of Boilermakers and Iron and Steel Shipbuilders organized the majority of the hull-construction trades,

---

[4] See Fig. 4.1 for fluctuations in world output of ships during this period. See Table A.2 for fluctuations in shipbuilding output in the Loire-Inférieure between 1900 and 1936.

[5] See Reid (1980: ch. 2) for a detailed account of the 19th-cent. development of trade-unionism in British shipbuilding.

and numerically was the most important of the shipyard unions, accounting for some 30 per cent of the manual work-force.[6] Initially based on skilled platers, angle-iron smiths, and riveters, the society pursued a policy of extending its organization to certain of the less-skilled and potentially competing metal-working trades, incorporating caulkers in 1874, holders-up in 1882, and a Clyde-based organization of sheet-iron-workers in 1896 (Mortimer 1973: 109, 134; Reid 1980: 144–7).

Second in numerical importance amongst the hull-construction trades was the SSA which, including loftsmen, accounted for about 10 per cent of the manual work-force. During the era of wooden ship-construction shipwrights had been the dominant trade in the production process. With the transition to iron and later to steel construction, however, they initially refused to work with the new material and later were supplanted by the boiler-maker trades as the principal occupational group. By the turn of the century shipwrights were relegated to mould-loft work, laying the keel, erecting and fairing the frames, launching the vessel, and to laying wooden flooring (Dougan 1975: 3; Reid 1980: 84).

In 1900 there were four competing unions organizing smiths: the Associated Blacksmiths' Society (about 3,000 members); the National United Society of Smiths and Hammermen (about 1,000 members) the United Kingdom Society of Associated Smiths and Strikers (about 4,300 members) and the Newcastle Co-operative Society (about 1,000 members). Between 1912 and 1914 a series of amalgamations led to their fusion into one society (Tuckett 1974: 70–2, 137–52). Smiths and their assistant hammermen constituted about 4 per cent of the work-force.

There were a large and diverse group of craft-unions catering to the various outfitting trades. The largest occupational group was joiners and carpenters comprising about 8 per cent of the work-force. This group was organized primarily by the Amalgamated Society of Carpenters and Joiners (Reid 1980: 187–90). Plumbers were grouped in a loose organization, the United Operative Plumbers' Association, and electricians were organized

---

[6] The %age figures are taken from Reid (1980: 442) and are based on the numbers employed at Harland and Wolff in Belfast in 1892. They exclude draughtsmen and patternmakers.

by the Electrical Trades Union formed in 1889 (Reid 1980: 173). Painters were mostly in the National Society of House and Ship Painters, though some were organized by the general labourers' unions (Clegg 1964: 47). The proportion of the work-force composed by outfitting trades varied between yards, being relatively high in yards engaged in liner or Admiralty work. At Harland and Wolff in 1892, a yard normally engaged in the production of large liners or warships, these trades accounted for slightly less than 20 per cent of the manual work-force.

The unskilled labourers and assistants were less well organized and only succeeded in forming permanent organizations during the boom of the late 1880s and early 1890s. The most important were the Tyneside and National Labourers' Union, with a strong base among platers' helpers, and the National Union of Gas-Workers and General Labourers (Clegg 1964: 25, 38–41). At the turn of the century the unskilled trades constituted about 40 per cent of the manual work-force.[7]

Conflict over the allocation of jobs and the right to man machines frequently resulted in sectional strikes. These were of two principal sorts: demarcation strikes between groups of skilled workers over the allocation of work; and dilution disputes provoked by the efforts of the employers to substitute less skilled grades on the traditional work of skilled workers. The intensification of these disputes during the second half of the nineteenth century was clearly related to the development of trade-unionism and collective bargaining. Such conflicts only became endemic to the industry with the strengthening of trade-union institutions and controls during the 1880s and 1890s, as each society attempted to secure or perhaps enlarge its share of the available work. Only a few of the more prominent conflicts will be mentioned here.

The Boilermakers' Society, which organized platers, angle-iron smiths, caulkers, riveters, and holders-up, became involved in demarcation conflicts with the SSA over the fairing of plates and

---

[7] This figure has remained roughly constant during the 20th cent. In 1936 the skilled apprenticed trades constituted 64% of the manual work-force in firms attached to the SEF (SRNA Archives, Part 1, No. 10, File 4092). The figure rested at 67% in 1960 for all shipbuilding firms in Great Britain. See Ministry of Labour and National Services Employment Exchange (1960).

the making of templates for plates. These conflicts intensified during the latter half of the 1890s (Reid 1980: 148–9). The Boilermakers also disputed the rights to angle-iron smithy work with the Blacksmiths and the Engineers and became involved in jurisdictional disputes with an independent drillers' union. In the latter case the efforts of the drillers to be admitted into the Boilermakers' Society as a trade group were consistently rebuffed, which eventually led the drillers into a merger with the SSA in 1910 (Mortimer 1973: 159–60; Reid 1980: 146–7; Tuckett 1974: 83–4). The Boilermakers also became embroiled in dilution conflict with the platers' helpers following the simplification of plating work in the 1880s (Mortimer 1973: 110–11; Reid 1980: 117–21). Amongst the outfitting trades, notable disputes were those between the Plumbers' Association and the Society of Engineers over copper-piping work and those between the SSA and the Society of Carpenters and Joiners over wooden fittings. The latter disputes intensified during the 1880s (Dougan 1975: 62–5; Reid 1980: 174–5).

Further, as the less skilled formed their own organizations during the 1890s, there was a tendency for these unions to adopt a strategy similar to that of the craft-unions, acting to limit access to particular jobs. The National Labourers' Union became involved in jurisdictional disputes with the National Union of Gas-Workers in the yards on the north-east coast and disputed the rights to painting with the House and Ship Painters' Society on the Clyde (Clegg 1964: 47).

Union-imposed restrictions clearly constrained the employers' ability to reorganize the division of labour and introduce new machinery. In particular, the skilled unions had considerable success in preventing the employers from exploiting the possibilities which technical change offered for substituting less skilled and lower paid workers for skilled workers.[8] A prime example of this is provided by the outcome of a series of conflicts over the introduction of pneumatic machinery shortly after 1900. In the

---

[8] A. Reid (1980: 223–4) persuasively argues that the Boilermakers, and other unions in the industry affected by mechanization, tended to adopt nationally co-ordinated policies in an effort to limit dilution and secure their position in the shipyard division of labour.

case of pneumatic riveting machines, the Boilermakers' Society enforced the use of a full squad of four on the new equipment despite the need for only three, and also resisted any reduction in piece rates below hand-work rates. While the Boilermakers' Society conceded reductions in hand-rates for pneumatic caulking and drilling equipment, they were able to limit the employers' use of lower paid apprentice labour.[9]

It would be misleading to conclude, however, that the effects of unionization were solely negative as far as employers were concerned. Unionization conferred important benefits in both the organization of production and cyclical flexibility in hiring and firing.

By the 1860s the process of abolishing outdoor relief for unemployed able-bodied males which had begun with the passage of the Poor Law Amendment Act in 1834 was substantially complete. The state's withdrawal from the provision of these social-welfare benefits prompted workers to insure themselves against loss of income through trade unions and friendly societies (Boyer 1988). The principal unions organizing in the shipbuilding industry provided a variety of forms of insurance, including unemployment, sick, and superannuation pay (Dougan 1975: 130, 196, 205; Mortimer 1973: 22–3, 42, 93; Mortimer 1982: 17, 128).

The provision of such social-welfare services by the unions was key to the success of British shipbuilding since it maintained the attachment of skilled workers to the shipbuilding districts during periods of recession. Further, the geographically based union branches not only increased the efficiency of labour-markets by acting as local labour exchanges, but also facilitated the movement of labour between regions through the provision of tramping benefit (Mortimer 1973: 42).

The unions also contributed to the provision of skills and the co-ordination of the work process. The skilled metal-workers were organized on the squad system whereby a group of skilled workers contracted for tasks such as a row of plates. The squads took responsibility for co-ordinating the production process on

---

[9] See Lorenz (1984: 618–21) for a detailed account of these conflicts. For similar conflicts between the ASE and the Engineering Employers' Federation at the turn of the century, see Zeitlin (1982).

the shop floor and for supervising their semi-skilled assistants. This reduced the need for bureaucratic planning of production and for specialized managerial personnel to supervise the mannual work-force (Holms 1918: 473, 527).

The work-force acquired its skills through a system of apprenticeship that was administered by the unions. Apprentices were paid well below the fully skilled rate during the five-year indenture period which in general was adhered to. The relatively low pay of apprentices allowed employers to recoup their initial investments in training in an industry where skills were for the most part industry-specific.[10]

The contrast with France is illustrative of the important role played by craft-unionism in sustaining the competitiveness of British shipbuilding. The first evidence of union organization in the Loire-Inférieure dates from the 1880s with the formation in Saint-Nazaire of the Chambre syndicale des forgerons et aides (smith and hammermen) with about ninety members; and a multi-craft-union, the Chambre syndical des corporations réunies, with about sixty members (Barbance 1948: 501–2). By the mid-1890s there were ten craft-unions in Saint-Nazaire with a combined membership of 588. In Nantes there were eleven unions at this time, organizing 664 workers. The expansion of trade-unionism was continuous in each town, though more rapid in Saint-Nazaire, where by 1907 three additional unions had been formed and the combined membership had increased by slightly less than fourfold to 1,911 members. In Nantes in 1907 unions organized 918 workers (Archives nationales, Paris, Series F7 13606).

The percentage of shipyard workers unionized at this time in the Loire-Inférieure can only be roughly estimated due to the lack of a good series of figures on the number of employees in the yards. It is clear that craft-unionism was weak by British standards and that conditions did not approach the closed shop. Drawing on a number of sources, it can be estimated that be-

[10] Elbaum (1989) argues that the more than doubling of earnings which typically followed the completion of apprenticeship lines in British engineering at the turn of the century cannot be accounted for by the difference between this value and the value of apprentice marginal product net of training costs during the final years of indenture. He argues that the strength of apprenticeship in British engineering allowed employers and workers to make credible commitments for stability of employment. This permitted employers to make initial investments in skills that were for the most part industry-specific.

tween 10 and 15 per cent of shipyard workers were unionized in Nantes and somewhat over 30 per cent in Saint-Nazaire.[11]

Lacking a developed network of craft-unions that might have provided social-welfare benefits as in Britain, French employers relied on other solutions to the problem of retaining an adequate work-force. One possible response to demand-instability was to shift trained labour into alternative employment during periods of recession. For example, in the Marseille region there is evidence that builders maintained shipyard factories (*usines navales*) in related branches of industry such as locomotive and boiler production. Skilled workers were transferred to these sites during periodic slumps (Roux-Freissineng 1929: 34).

In the case of the Loire-Inférieure, there is no evidence that employers maintained *usines navales*. Rather, a solution emerged involving a unique symbiosis between agriculture and industry. When the Chantiers Penhoët was first set up in Saint-Nazaire in 1860 by John Scott and Co. of Greenock, Scotland under contract from the Compagnie générale transatlantique, the firm drew on peasant labour from the neighbouring parish of Brière, whose families continued to cultivate family plots (Barbance 1948: 367, 493). Reflecting back on his experiences in France in the 1860s during the meetings of the 1886 Royal Commission on Depression of Trade, J. Scott noted that some three to four hundred of his work-force would absent themselves three times a year from the yard: in the sowing period, the reaping period, and in the summer to cut peat (Royal Commission on Depression in Trade 1886, 3rd Report: 192–3).

In Saint-Nazaire and Nantes, as in other parts of provincial France, a section of the labour force retained its attachment to ·

[11] In Nantes, just prior to 1914, average employment in the three principal yards was about 4,500: Chantiers de la Loire (3,000); Chantiers de Bretagne (1,155); Chantiers Dubigeon (380). See Guin (1976: 377). In 1907 the Coueron foundry and the Basse-Indre smithy works each employed 800. See Thebault (1979: 74–5). The two principal engineering works were Voruz, and Buissoneau and Lotz. Including these, and the various smaller engineering establishments, total employment in the metal-transformation sector in Nantes is likely to have been in the range of 9,000 to 10,000, putting the %age unionized at about 10. In Saint-Nazaire, Chantiers de la Loire employed between 1,200 and 1,600 at the turn of the century, while Chantiers de l'Atlantique employed 4,500 during the 1900–1 boom, but only 3,900 in 1911. See Barbance (1948: 373, 386). With associated engineering works total employment for the metal-transformation trades is likely to have varied between 5,500 and 6,500, putting the %age unionized between 30 and 35.

the land. These workers were really half peasant, half wage-labourer, and they developed neither the degree of organization nor sense of working-class consciousness that characterized workers in Britain. While these features of the French labour-market have frequently been noted, the fact that they continued to characterize France well into the twentieth century is less well known. In 1920 the peasants from Brière, who still formed an important part of the shipyard work-force in Saint-Nazaire, were still leaving the yards during the summer to cut peat (Barbance 1948: 556).

This solution to maintaining a supply of skilled labour reflected the region's economic and social structure. With peasant proprietorship not only a viable but arguably a preferred alternative to industrial employment, the shipyards could only permanently attract workers to industrial employment if they could offer a standard of living at least as attractive as the agricultural alternative. Severe instability in shipbuilding output and employment precluded this, and consequently builders were pushed into drawing periodically on the underemployed fringes of the agricultural work-force.

The contrast between the patterns of labour mobility in the British and French shipbuilding industries leads to some general reflections on the conditions for the development of an effective system of craft labour-markets as characterized many regions of the British economy. First, the existence of a large number of firms in the industrial region or district. This lowered the probability that all firms' relative demand for particular types of skills would be the same at any one time. An individual employer could use a 'hire and fire' policy without risking permanent loss of skilled labour for the district, as it was generally possible for a worker to find comparable employment in another firm. Secondly, the dominance of the industry in the particular district. The absence of a viable alternative (such as agriculture in many French regions) reinforced workers' dependence on and commitment to the industry. Thirdly, a developed network of craft-unions. This facilitated the flow of labour between firms in a district and helped assure the work-force's attachment to the industry during periods of economic recession.

In the absence of such economic and institutional conditions, if production is to be maintained, alternative solutions to the problem of labour supply consistent with the characteristics of the industry have to be found. The unique symbiosis between agriculture and industry in the shipbuilding district of the Loire-Inférieure was one such alternative.

IV. Scientific Management

The symbiosis between agriculture and industry in the Loire-Inférieure helped maintain the supply of skilled labour for shipbuilders. But this posed a further set of problems. Not only were the seasonal migrations of labour between industry and agriculture not necessarily in phase with the cyclical demands of the shipbuilding industry, but the French peasant/worker was inevitably less specialized and habituated to the needs of industry than his British counterpart. It was in this context that French producers began to look for changes in the organization of work that would concentrate the more responsible technical and supervisory tasks in a small cadre of employees enjoying more stable employment (Barbance 1948: 389; Benoist 1905: 330–43). In this manner they acted to economize on their need for skilled manual labour.

This point can be illustrated by contrasting the templating systems used in French and British yards. Templates were wooden models or replicas used to mark plates for hole-punching and shearing. There were two basic types of templates: transferring and pattern. The former were relatively crude and simple, being prepared by platers who would press flexible wooden battens against the surface of the partially constructed hull to determine the shape of plates and the positioning of rivet-holes. Pattern templates were more precise and elaborate, having rivet-holes bored in them and showing the exact dimensions of sections. These were made in advance of the start of construction by loftsmen on the basis of the designs and information supplied by draughtsmen (Holms 1918: ch. 36).

In terms of the allocation of skills and technical expertise, the use of transferring templates left manual workers in control of determining the disposition of conjoined parts and connecting rivet-holes, technical tasks requiring basic production engineering skills (Holms 1918: 486–8). In the pattern templating system, these technical tasks were separated from the shop floor and concentrated in the design offices and mould-loft, the responsibility of employees whose competencies were primarily technical. Further, the small-scale draught plans prepared by the design staff had to be more detailed in this case, providing sufficient information so that mould-loft personnel could transform them into accurate large-scale drawings of the components which would serve as a basis for producing templates.

In France, from the evidence available, the full pattern templating system was in use in certain yards prior to 1914 and was quite general during inter-war years (Benoist 1905: 330–43; Barbance 1948: 388; Pinczon 1930: 92–4). In Britain, however, while pattern templates were used for certain midship plates and connecting angles where repeat work was possible, the majority of plates were prepared from transferring templates which the plating squads were responsible for constructing (Holms 1918: 486–8; Montgomerie 1937–8: 156–8, D80–1, 85). In effect, the connection between technical tasks and manual tasks was managed in quite different ways in Britain and France, the two being more clearly distinguished and separated in France.[12]

During World War I there was a further development of these tendencies towards the separation of technical tasks from manual work in French yards as the munitions sector came under state control. The need for an intensified pace of production under conditions of severe labour shortage led to systematic efforts to apply Taylor's methods of scientific management to the shipyards of Nantes and Saint-Nazaire (Barbance 1948: 540–1; Guin 1976: 382; Fleury 1980: 547).[13] In 1916 Charles de Fremin-

---

[12] See Van Donkelaar (1932: 269–70) for the use of the full pattern templating system in Dutch shipbuilding during the inter-war period. For the use of the system more generally on the Continent during the inter-war years, see Montgomerie (1937–8: 153–76, and the discussion following the paper, *passim*).

[13] State-supported initiatives led to the application of Taylor's system in the gunpowder, shell and ordnance, general metallurgy, and marine engineering industries during the war. See the series of reports in the *Bulletin de la société d'encouragement pour l'industrie nationale* (1919). Also see Devinat (1927: 233–8).

ville, technical director of the Pemhard and Levassor works from 1899 to 1916 and an early proponent of Taylor's system in France, was called in to oversee the reorganization of Chantiers de l'Atlantique in Saint-Nazaire (Barbance 1948: 439; Devinat 1927: 235–6).

The rationalization began in the design office.[14] The designs for individual pieces were set out in greater detail and schedules for the maximum and minimum allowable tolerances in the execution of a piece were established. Attempts were made to simplify individual pieces for production in series, though these efforts proved of little worth due to the customized nature of ship production.

Secondly, the Nomenclature Service was established, whose role was to identify the sequence of operations in the fabrication of a component. The absence of flow diagrams had led to disruptions in production, especially in the case of new types of components. Each section of a vessel was reduced to its components and the successive stages of machining were specified up to the point of final assembly.

The Time Study Service was responsible for the overall organization of the labour process. The service determined allocated times for each individual job. Each job was broken down into its successive operations and the times spent in preparation, manual execution, and automatic-machine execution were distinguished. The allocated times were determined by time-studies performed by recruits to the service, drawn from the ranks of foremen, leading hands, and skilled men in the various shops. These 'time-setters' were divided into four sections: fitting, pipe-work, plating, and woodwork. Their offices were located at a distance from the shops in order to avoid pressure from the workers in the setting of times.

Earnings were based on a system of payment by results (*travail au marchandage*). Each worker was assigned a minimum hourly rate in accordance with his classification. A superior rate was earned when the worker spent fewer hours on a job than the

[14] The following description of the application of scientific management in the Atlantique yard is based on the account of L. Lavalée (1919), one of the yard's engineers.

allocated number.[15] Times determined on the basis of studies
were automatically increased: preparation time by 40 per cent;
manual-execution time by 10 per cent; and machining time by 10
per cent. This was to allow for unpredictable disruptions in the
flow of work (Barbance 1948: 590).

In certain cases individual contracts were worked, but generally the system was applied to groups of between twenty and a
hundred workers. For complex jobs group leaders were assigned
instruction sheets detailing operations in a step-by-step way, spe-
cifying the speeds to employ in machining a piece and the means
of obtaining these speeds. All group leaders completed follow-up
forms which indicated the number of workers on a contract, the
allocated time for the job, and the percentage bonus for the
group. On the basis of these forms the Manpower Office calcu-
lated the overall bonus for each worker.

Each month the Time Study Service would determine the average bonus by trade and by work-group, deciding whether it was
too low or too high, and would make appropriate adjustments. A
careful examination of the level of bonus payments allowed the
service to determine where disruptions had occurred in the production process. An abnormally low bonus might indicate supply
bottle-necks or alternatively deficiencies in a particular work-
group. In this manner the study of the bonuses provided a means
to identify problems that otherwise might have escaped attention.

The co-ordination of production from above was encouraged
by the lack of skilled labour in France, a condition which
precluded the use of indirect forms of control based on the
semi-autonomous work-group or squad as in Britain. The British

[15] The bonus as a %age of the time-rate was determined by the following
formula: bonus % $= \dfrac{(T - t)\ 100}{t}$ where T = allocated time and t = time spent.
This payment system relates the time-rate to piecework payment by stipulating a
level of output to be produced in a given time to qualify for the time-rate and
paying a higher rate proportionately as this output level is exceeded. As is typical
with such systems, the tendency of employers to decrease the allocated times if too
large a bonus was earned encouraged workers to restrict their output. To overcome this problem many employers in Nantes and Saint-Nazaire applied the
regressive Rowan system, which paid a lower overall rate for a piece the quicker it
was completed, though a higher hourly rate. The bonus was determined
as formula: bonus % $= \dfrac{(T - t)\ 100}{T}$. See Dubigeon (1928: 22–31).

system relied on the interdependency between and general knowledge of squad members. For example, while skilled platers specialized in templating, shearing, bending, or furnacing, each had a working knowledge of the other members' responsibilities and tasks and consequently could co-ordinate his own work in relation to that of his squad partners without the need of higher level supervision or instruction. Broader knowledge was the precondition for workable specialization independent of managerial control.

It was precisely this form of indirect control over production which the shortage of skilled labour in French shipbuilding regions precluded. To overcome these problems employers acted to concentrate technical tasks amongst a small cadre of technical workers as evidenced by the use of pattern-templating methods. This was a pre-condition for the development of more systematic methods of management as evidenced in the use of scientific management after 1914. Taylorism should be seen as an extension of tendencies already at work in the French shipyard production process.

V. The Craft System versus Scientific Management

I have argued in this chapter that the more systematic co-ordination of production from above and the emphasis on technical and supervisory services in France reflected economic and institutional conditions which resulted in scarce supplies of skilled labour for large-scale industrial employers. If this is a valid line of reasoning, then we would expect like trends in other industries with similar technological characteristics: mechanical and heavy engineering.

There are difficulties with pursuing this line of inquiry since detailed comparative and historical studies do not exist to show such subtle differences as those between the systems of templating described here. It may be possible to proceed in a somewhat more indirect manner, though, through an interpretation of the relative receptiveness of industrialists in Britain and France to F. W. Taylor's system of scientific management prior to and during World War I. In considering the question from this angle, it is important not to overestimate the practical importance of the scientific management movement in any country prior to 1914. In France, Taylor's works were widely read with the appearance of translations, sponsored by Le Chatelier, of *Shop Management* in 1907 and *The Principles of Scientific Management* in 1911 (Devinat 1927: 211–16, 232–45; Heron 1975; Moutet 1975). Applications remained few and scattered prior to the war, though, the most fruitful sector being the car industry. The war-years saw a considerable increase in the number of applications, particularly in the state-controlled munitions sector.[16]

Though the balance sheet of applications in France is not impressive, the contrast with Britain is none the less striking. Not only is there no evidence of applications in British industry prior to the war, but also opinion among industrialists, in sharp contrast to France, ranged from apathy to hostility (Littler 1980; Urwick and Brech 1946: 88–136). The *Engineer*, one of the two principal voices of the engineering world, took a distinctly adverse stance (Levine 1967: 60–8).

There are a number of reasons for this conservatism. Anticipated labour resistance was no doubt an important factor. The major practical consideration must have been the widespread and largely successful use at this time of indirect forms of labour control based on some modification of the internal contract system. In the case of the shipbuilding industry, it was the metal-working squads who organized the details of hull construction and supervised the unskilled. Similar arrangements could be found in the textile, mechanical and heavy engineering, automobile, and glass industries (Littler 1980: 162–3). Well into the twentieth century many British industrialists remained highly dependent on their skilled workers for shop-floor control and organization.

From the perspective of the structure of the French economy as a whole, the greater interest of industrialists during the late

---

[16] According to P. Fridenson (1978), 1% of French manufacturing firms applied a version of scientific management prior to the war. For applications in the car industry, see De Ram (1909) and Laux (1972). For other pre-war applications, see Abaut (1913) and the studies summarized by Le Chatelier and de Freminville in the *Bulletin de la société d'encouragement pour l'industrie nationale* (1914). For wartime applications, see the series of reports by Nusbaumer, Compagnon, Lavalée, Lecler, and Charpy in the same journal (1919).

nineteenth and early twentieth centuries in systematic methods of management may seem surprising. It is generally accepted that France's industrial structure was highly fragmented. In 1906 establishments with less than ten employees accounted for 56 per cent of the industrial work-force, in 1926 for 41 per cent, and even in 1936 for 39 per cent (Levy-Leboyer 1976: 98). This indicates the importance of petty-proprietor modes of production in which bureaucratic systems of management would be unlikely to play a role.

Recent research suggests that it is more appropriate to view the French economy as having a dual structure, rather than a uniformly more decentralized one than its competitors. If we restrict our attention to the largest firms (more than 1,000 employees) in such sectors as shipbuilding, engineering, and metal transformation, the average size of firms in terms of number of employees is comparable to Britain, the United States, or Germany. What distinguishes the French economy from others is the relative importance and continued vitality of small-scale artisanal forms of production (Caron 1974: 98–104; Levy-Leboyer 1976: 98; O'Brien and Keyder 1978: 160–8). Consequently, it is not particularly surprising that only a small percentage of firms attempted to adopt a version of scientific management, since these efforts were restricted to the larger firms, primarily in mechanical engineering and metal transformation.

It was argued above that the strength of peasant proprietorship in France allowed the land to absorb additional labour during the nineteenth century, limiting the supply to industry. The other important pole of attraction in France was petty proprietorship, the vitality of which promised an alternative to factory employment. To a considerable extent, what was at stake here was a question of values and preferences. As T. Kemp (1962: 341) has noted, independent proprietorship had a considerable allure:

The hereditary proletariat in such fields (small workshops) was not an industrial worker of the modern type but had more affinity with old handicraftsmen; politically he turned to Proudhon rather than Marx. Where other conditions were favourable for the establishment of factory production, employers found it difficult to recruit and discipline the labour force which they required. Factory labour for a long time was regarded as degrading, fit only for the more proverty stricken fringes of the rural population who made up the immigrants to the towns.

While the interest of large-scale industrialists in systematic management techniques from the late nineteenth century onwards in France probably stemmed from the problem of scarce supplies of skilled labour, this is not to ignore that Taylorism was instituted to strengthen managerial control over the shop floor and to increase the intensity of work-effort. In the case of shipbuilding, the evidence available for the Chartiers de l'Atlantique yard in Saint-Nazaire shows that labour productivity increased following the introduction of the system. Yet scientific management was far from being ideally suited to the industry. Time-studies at the Chartiers de l'Atlantique had to be substantially redone for each contract and many jobs went untimed (Barbance 1948: 449–50). Certainly French builders in Nantes and Saint-Nazaire achieved no increases in productivity that provided them with a competitive edge over British builders who continued to rely on less formal methods of work administration (see Ch. 1).

The underlying reasons for this have been identified in a seminal article by A. L. Stinchcombe (1959–60) on the construction industry which shares many of the shipbuilding industry's distinctive market and technical features. Stinchcombe argues that bureaucratization of work administration depends on long-term stability of work-flows. Only under this condition will the overheads associated with the firm-specific information-processing channels, which are required to operate bureaucratic systems, be sufficiently productive to make them economical. The flexible British system of craft-production, which economized on these overheads, was successful in shipbuilding largely because the product was non-standard and firm output levels were highly variable. The generally trained British workers were easily able to adapt to an ever-changing product mix without the need for upper-level supervision. They also were able to move between yards in a district as firm output levels varied (see Ch. 2).

This interpretation of the basis for British competitive success in the craft system of organization suggests an understanding of the system as a set of institutions that were retained because of their efficiency properties and the mutual benefits they generated for skilled workers and their employers. While the craft system undoubtedly had advantages over more bureaucratic systems and produced joint benefits, this did not preclude conflict between the principal actors. Not only were there serious differences between the employers and skilled workers over questions of machine-manning, but also disputes between competing groups of skilled workers over the allocation work. This suggests that the craft system in British shipbuilding, rather than being an equilibrium solution to the problem of finding the most efficient way to organize production, should be seen as a political *compromise*, where each actor recognized that the others had an interest in sustaining the system, but also an interest in shifting the terms of the agreement to their advantage.[17]

This conception of interests, as being neither entirely the same nor entirely conflicting, was reflected in and reinforced by the history of sectional disputes in the industry. The metal-working trades in the Boilermakers' Society, for example, worked in close proximity with members of the SSA engaged in pattern-making and hull assembly. There was an obvious mutual dependence. Yet the Boilermakers had only achieved their dominant position in the industry by displacing woodworking shipwrights during the transition from wooden to iron construction after 1860 (Pollard and Robertson 1979: 153). Similarly, co-operative relations between the employers and the Boilermakers were punctuated by conflicts over the employers' efforts to stock the industry with cheaper apprentice labour (Lorenz 1984: 618–20). The effect of such disputes was to generate a high degree of *distrust* over any proposed change in institutional arrangements that threatened to alter the established division of labour between groups of skilled workers or between the skilled and less skilled.

I argue in Chapter 5 that these distrusting beliefs constituted a serious liability for the industry after World War II when its survival depended on a mutually agreed process of institutional reform. Before addressing this, I describe in Chapter 4 the changes in market conditions and technology that progressively undermined Britain's comparative advantage in shipbuilding by shifting the competitive edge to yards employing bureaucratic methods of work administration.

---

[17] The conception of the firm as compromise is developed more fully in Ch. 5.

4

Industry Structure and Competitive Decline, 1948–1970

THE chronology of British shipbuilding decline presented in Chapter 1 identified the decade following World War II as a key turning-point in the industry's competitive fortunes. The more than twofold increase in world output of the 1950s saw the proportion of ships built in Britain cut from 40 per cent to 15 per cent. During the 1960s, while world demand expanded at an unprecedented rate, the British industry sustained an absolute decline with the closure of a number of the major yards. By the end of the 1960s Britain accounted for about 5 per cent of world output, ranking fourth behind Japan, Sweden, and West Germany.

The British shipbuilding industry depended on government support for its survival during the 1960s. This began in 1963 with the provision of loans at low interest rates for new construction. The 1967 Shipbuilding Industry Act authorized direct grants of up to £5 million to yards participating in a proposed restructuring scheme calling for the formation of regional shipbuilding consortia. By 1971 £42.9 million had been provided in grants and loans to builders. Other government departments (principally the Department of Trade and Industry and the Ministry of Defence (Naval)) had provided a further £116.8 million by 1972 (Hogwood 1979: 87–93). By the early 1970s the level of direct and indirect assistance received by British producers compared favourably with that of producers in Japan or on the Continent. Despite this, the position of many British firms remained precarious. While the industry's absolute decline was arrested, there was a further loss of market share during the 1970s (Booz-Allen and Hamilton Report 1973: 59–61).

The declining post-war fortunes of the British shipbuilding

industry took place during a period of technical change and sharply changing demand conditions. In short order, the composition of the world fleet was transformed, moving towards larger and more standardized vessels, and welding and pre-fabrication techniques were substituted for traditional shipbuilding technology. These changes in turn encouraged investment in larger scale and more mechanized shipbuilding facilities.

While these post-war changes transformed the British industry as abroad, their impact was comparatively modest prior to the government-sponsored restructuring programme of the late 1960s. The tonnage produced annually and the degree of mechanization of production were on average less in British shipyards during the 1950s and 1960s than in the yards of such major competitors as Sweden, Japan, and France. In this chapter I discuss the economic and technical changes that transformed the world shipbuilding industry after World War II, and I offer some reasons for the comparatively piecemeal modernization of the British industry structure.

I. Product-Market and Technical Change in World Shipbuilding

The rapid growth of industrialized nations after World War II resulted in an unprecedented expansion of sea-borne trade and the world fleet. Between 1950 and 1970 the volume of sea-borne trade increased from 510 million to 2,530 million tons or at a compound annual rate of 7.9 per cent. As shown in Table 4.1, during the same period the world fleet increased from 85.3 to 215 million gross tons or at a compound annual rate of 4.6 per cent.[1]

This expansion in the demand for shipping services resulted in rather spectacular increases in world output of ships. Between

---

[1] This difference between the rates of growth of the world fleet and world trade is an indication of the increases in shipping efficiency that have been achieved due to increases in speed, improvement in harbour facilities, and the increase in the dead weight to gross tonnage ratio as vessels have increased in size. Between 1953 and 1973 the average dead weight to gross tonnage ratio for all vessels increased from 1.40 to 1.66. See Drewry (1974). See App. B for the distinction between dead weight and gross tons.

TABLE 4.1. World dry cargo and tanker fleets (millions of gross tons)

Year	Tanker	Dry cargo	Total
1950	18.6	66.7	85.3
1960	41.7	100.2	141.9
1970	88.2	126.8	215.0

Source: Lloyd's Register of Shipping, Annual Shipbuilding Returns.

1950 and 1970 world tonnage launched increased from 3.25 to 21 million gross tons. Further, as shown in Figure 4.1, growth in world ship production was comparatively stable during this period, the fall in output during the 1958–62 recession being slight in comparison with those of the recessions prior to 1939.

The expanding world market for ships after World War II was comparatively international in character, unlike the pre-1914 period, which was characterized by a close integration between national fleets and national producers. After 1950 there was a rapid expansion of flags of convenience such as Liberia and Panama, as well as the expansion of the Greek and Norwegian fleets which benefited from little or no domestic shipbuilding capacity. Between 1950 and 1970 export orders accounted for some 40 to 45 per cent of the tonnage launched in the world (see Table A.3). To a much greater extent than in the past, the success of producing nations during this period depended on their ability to compete in international markets.[2]

As Table 4.2 indicates, the post-war expansion was accompanied by a growth in the average size of vessels, though this tendency was less pronounced in Britain than in her major competitors. This increase in average vessel size was particularly pronounced in the case of the specialized oil-carrying tanker fleet, which emerged as the most dynamic sector of the market

---

[2] The figures on exports are somewhat exaggerated, since nationals of shipbuilding countries may register ships under flags of convenience. As Parkinson (1960: 91) has correctly pointed out, though, 'Much of the tonnage registered (under flags of convenience) is owned by international shipping operators to whom it is a matter of indifference where ships are purchased provided that they represent good value for money, and in consequence the markets of Liberia and Panama provide a better opportunity of assessing the competitive position of the main shipbuilding countries than their performance in home markets.'

Fɪɢ. 4.1. Tonnage launched in the world (log scale)
(000s of gross tons)

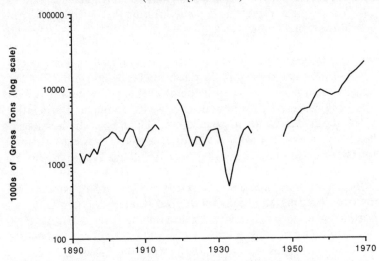

Source: Lloyd's Register of Shipping, Annual Shipbuilding Returns.

Tᴀʙʟᴇ 4.2. Average size of vessels over 100 gross tons under
construction

	Tankers				Non-Tankers			
1950	11,818	14,839	9,462	1,500	3,855	4,319	1,770	2,092
1955	13,265	21,919	11,683	3,659	4,429	3,150	3,751	5,356
1960	17,533	27,002	23,091	3,145	4,187	5,166	4,750	4,490
1965	30,369	38,407	32,918	38,799	5,810	3,162	9,417	11,505
1970	30,578	111,905	63,520	62,015	9,090	9,330	12,574	11,440

Source: Lloyd's Register of Shipping, Annual Shipbuilding Returns.

after the war. Between 1950 and 1970 the world tanker fleet increased from 16.9 to 86.1 million gross tons. Tankers accounted for 47 per cent of total tons launched during the 1950s and 57 per cent during the 1960s.

Another significant tendency after World War II was the growing acceptance in the world market for standard tankers, bulk-carriers, and cargo vessels. Swedish and Japanese firms led the way in pursuing a strategy of batch production of standard vessels after the war, which some British yards emulated during the 1960s. Individual yards in Sweden and Japan typically adopted a flexible strategy of offering a limited range of standard designs for tankers and bulk-carriers (Ollson 1981*a* and 1981*b*; Parkinson 1960: 150, 182–3, 215).

Producing standard vessels in series or alternatively concentrating on producing large tankers offered producers potentially important gains in productivity when combined with the new high throughput technology of the post-World War II era. The essential elements of this new technology were the use of arc welding in place of riveting for joining pieces, the substitution of oxy-acetylene burning for the traditional combination punching and shearing machine, and the use of prefabrication of sections of the hull in place of piece-by-piece assembly at the berth.

The techniques of arc and oxy-acetylene welding[3] date from considerably before World War II, though their use in shipbuilding was quite limited before that time, being restricted primarily to boiler and hull repairs and to ship's fittings such as pipe-joints or flange connections.[4] During the 1920s the poor quality of

---

[3] In arc welding, used primarily for heavy structural work, the heat for the fusion of the connecting pieces is provided by an electric arc which passes between a flux-covered electrode and the parent plate melting both plates and the tip of the electrode to deposit what is called a 'weld pool'. As the electrode passes along the joint the pool solidifies to form a bond. In gas welding, used in lighter work, a fuel, usually acetylene, and oxygen are mixed in a torch and burnt to create a high-temperature flame. The process is usually used manually, the worker feeding a wire or rod into the weld pool for filler material as required.

[4] Bare-wire arc welding was developed around the turn of the century in both the USA and Russia. Arc welding was first used for hull repairs during the First World War. See Houldcroft (1973) for the technical and practical development of welding. The extensive use of welding on pipe-work by the inter-war years is evidenced by the agreements signed in Britain between the SEF and the United Operative Plumbers' Association determining conditions and rates for the use of arc and oxy-acetylene welding plant. SRNA Archives, Federation Circulars, 1920, *passim*.

electrodes and a concern over the possible brittle fracture of welded joints discouraged the use of arc welding for hull construction where parts were subject to considerable stress. The development of the covered electrode during the 1930s, which allowed for a greater reliability of welded connections, alleviated much of this concern (Parkinson 1960: 112; Haigh 1933).

The critical factor in the practical development of the technique in Britain and in a number of other nations was the naval construction programmes pursued during the 1930s, where welding was adopted as a weight-saving measure rather than a response to anticipated increases in labour productivity (Parkinson 1960: 113–16; Redshaw 1949). In Britain, the technique was initially introduced in the major warship construction yards such as Vickers-Armstrong, Cammell Laird, J. Samuel White, and Harland and Wolff. The limited practical importance of the technique in the British shipbuilding industry as a whole is reflected in employment returns for all firms attached to the SEF in 1936, which show that welders constituted less than 1 per cent of the manual work-force (SRNA Archives, Part I, No. 10, File 4092).[5]

During World War II there was an extension of welding in conjunction with gas-burning techniques, which proved more suitable for cutting plates as shearing machines gave an insufficiently precise edge for welding and required a further planing operation. The first automatic welding and burning machines were installed in Britain at this time. With few exceptions, the major firms in the industry invested in the automatic flame-planer or profile-burner during the period 1942–4 (SRNA Archives, Part II, No. 17, File 5007). Investment in the automatic Union Melt welding machine, though, was confined to a few firms, primarily the traditional naval and liner specialists.[6]

The extension of welding at this time was directly connected to the development of prefabrication which was generally limited to

[5] A Dec. 1936 report showed that welders were primarily concentrated in yards specializing in warship construction: Vickers-Armstrong, Harland and Wolff in Belfast, Cammell Laird, John Brown, and Hawthorne Leslie. The only cargo specialist with an appreciable number was Lithgows, at the Kingston yard. SRNA Archives, Part I, No. 10, File 4092.

[6] SRNA Archives, Part II, No. 17, File 5007. The Union Melt system was installed at Vickers-Armstrong, Cammell Laird, Barclay-Curle, John Brown, Lithgows' east yard, Schott's, J. Samuel White, and three unnamed Tyneside firms.

fairly small two-dimensional sections, usually weighing less than ten tons. Welding provided a practical incentive to the use of prefabrication. While welding can be done in the overhead, vertical, or downhand position, it is easiest to weld when the surface is flat and in the downhand position. In the case of mechanical welding, it is a practical requirement that the surface is flat and on the horizontal plane so that the welding unit can travel over it. These considerations encouraged the prefabrication of sections indoors, with suitable overhead cranage capacity to move sections into the ideal position for welding (Parkinson 1960: 120–1).

The development of prefabrication in Britain during the war was constrained firstly by the limited cranage capacity existing in yards, but more importantly by the need to avoid the inevitable dislocations to production that would have accompanied any major technical restructuring. Most firms, in applying prefabrication, made do with rather makeshift adaptations to the existing layout of their yards, for example by erecting portable shelters adjacent to berths to be used as welding skids.[7]

After the war, welding and burning techniques were generally introduced in Britain and by the mid-1950s had largely supplanted riveting and shearing. The size of prefabricated sections also increased during this period, to an average of about thirty tons by the end of the 1950s, though sections might occasionally weigh as much as 300 tons (Parkinson 1960: 121).

The development of prefabrication and welding resulted in a progressive abandoning of the traditional keel-up building procedure whereby individual plates and beams were shaped on a job-shop basis in the sheds and then erected and fitted piece by piece at the berth. The new procedure was to prefabricate large three-dimensional block sections of the vessel indoors, which were then transported by crane or rail to the berth and welded together. This new procedure encouraged the development of a flow conception of hull construction in which relatively simple standard components were built up into larger and more complex shapes.

---

[7] For wartime modifications to the layout of British yards, see Shepheard (1943–4: 159–60). A few yards, with Admiralty assistance, initiated major modernization schemes during the war. For the case of Vickers-Armstrong's Walker yard on the Tyne, see the *Shipbuilder and Marine Engine Builder* (March 1949: 168–74).

Certain firms in Britain initiated ambitious programmes of modernization immediately after the war designed to reorganize the layout of their yards to suit this flow concept. Plating sheds were enlarged and large prefabrication bays were constructed at the head of the berths, serviced by adequate cranage capacity to transport prefabricated sections.[8] These yards were the exceptions. The majority of firms in Britain did not invest on this scale during the late 1940s and early 1950s but, rather, made piecemeal modifications to the existing disposition of sheds and berths to allow for an extension of prefabrication (Parkinson 1960: 121–3).

With continuous increases in the popular sizes of commercial vessels, though, certain alterations in the size and disposition of berths became a practical necessity by the mid-1950s. This, and the increasing effectiveness of foreign competition based on more up-to-date methods, led to a more general technical restructuring in Britain after 1955 (Parkinson 1960: 123–5).[9]

It is difficult to estimate the savings in man-hours made by introducing prefabrication and welding techniques during the late 1940s and early 1950s, since it is generally impossible to separate out the savings attributable to the use of more capital-intensive techniques and those attributable to the routinization of the work which increasing standardization facilitated. Figures presented by K. Ollson (1981*b*: 13) on the decrease in the man-hours required to build a series of 18,000-ton tankers at the Eriksberg yard in Sweden give an indication of the combined effects. The vessels were produced between 1947 and 1954 when the system of prefabrication was being extended and perfected. Between the first and fifth vessel in the series, built in 1947 and 1951 respectively, man-hours fell by 20.5 per cent. By the time the twelfth tanker had been built in 1953 man-hours had fallen by a further 3.7 per cent.[10]

---

[8] For the early modernization of W. Doxford and Sons, Vickers-Armstrong's yard at Barrow-in-Furness, and the Lobnitz yard respectively, see Stephenson (1952); Redshaw (1947); Hagan (1946).

[9] See Department of Scientific and Industrial Research (1960) which notes that the industry rate of investment increased after 1955.

[10] Also see Rapping (1965: 81–6) for the productivity gains achieved in mass producing Liberty vessels during World War II in the USA. Rapping's figures show a remarkable 122% increase between Dec. 1941 and Dec. 1944, or an average annual gain of about 40%. The regression analysis carried out by Rapping suggests that over half of this can be attributed to the 'learning process'. The conditions, as he notes, were exceptional. Labour, with no prior experience in

The experience of producing standard vessels in series or specializing in producing very large tankers or bulk-carriers by means of assembly-line methods for hull construction, in which ships' hulls were built up from standard components. The basic idea was to produce on an automatic assembly line a large volume of standard rectangular boxes or panels. These were then prefabricated into larger block units which in turn were put together, like the pieces of a puzzle, to form the vessel's hull. This assembly-line technology, while offering potential improvements in productivity, was highly capital-intensive. It only proved profitable to install in yards specializing in supertanker production or in series production of standard cargo vessels or bulk-carriers, where the volume throughput of standard panels was high.[11] Its very limited use in Britain during the 1960s reflected both the lack of product standardization and the comparatively small tonnage throughput of most British yards (Cuthbert 1969: 123–4, 127–9; Forbes and Varney 1976: 39; Ollson 1981*b*; Wolfenden 1976: 67–8, 71).[12]

II. British Industry Structure: The Failure to Change

The adoption of high throughput technology in world shipbuilding after World War II can best be understood as a cumulative process.[13] The market success of producers in Japan, Sweden, and France, based on specializing their facilities for the produc-

shipbuilding, was placed under the direction of similarly inexperienced management. Figures presented by Stopford (1979) probably more accurately reflèct the gains typically derived from the learning process alone. Based on figures for series production of SD14 cargo ships at Austin and Pickersgill in Britain during the 1970s, Stopford estimated that a productivity gain of some 25% can be achieved over the first four or five vessels completed.

[11] The impact of this assembly-line technology on skill requirements is discussed in Ch. 5. The main advantage in producing large and relatively simple box-like vessels such as tankers and bulk-carriers is that the flat midship section of the vessel, which can be easily constructed from standard panels, is increased as a proportion of the entire hull surface.

[12] Stopford (1979) has estimated that investing in specialized capital equipment for series production or supertanker production can result in a savings in man-hours of 20 to 25% above the savings attributable to the learning effect.

[13] The argument in this section is based substantially on Lorenz and Wilkinson (1986: 119–24).

TABLE 4.3. Average output per yard and per firm in British, French, and Swedish mercantile shipbuilding, 1950–1970 (000s tons launched)

Country	Year	No. of		Average output		Total industry output
		yards	firms	per yard	per firm	
Britain	1950	58	46	24.1	28.8	1,324.6
	1960	52	43	25.6	30.9	1,331.5
	1970	40	27	30.9	45.8	1,237.1
France	1950	17	14	10.6	12.9	180.8
	1960	15	12	39.6	49.5	594.4
	1970	8	6	120.0	160.0	960.2
Sweden	1950	10	10	34.8	34.8	348.0
	1960	10	10	71.1	71.1	711.0
	1970	11	7	155.6	244.5	1,711.2

Note: The figures exclude boat-, barge-, and yacht-builders.

Sources: Industry output figures are from *Lloyd's Register of Shipping*, Annual Shipbuilding Returns. British figures: the *Shipbuilder and Marine Engineer* (Jan. nos. of each year). French figures: Puech (1969) and Chardonnet (1971). Swedish figures: *Projekt Svensk Varindustri*, Gothenberg.

tion of very large tankers or for series production of standard vessels, allowed them to invest profitably in this comparatively capital-intensive technology. The productivity gains and lower production costs which resulted in turn allowed them to expand their share of competitive international markets and achieve higher tonnage throughputs. By the mid-1950s specialized yards such as Kokums and Gotaverken in Sweden were producing annually between 70,000 and 100,000 tons. By 1960 it was not uncommon for large yards producing series of standard vessels to complete over 150,000 tons annually.

Table 4.3 shows the tendency towards larger tonnage throughput per yard in Britain, France, and Sweden between 1950 and 1970. The comparatively small increase in scale of production achieved on average by British shipbuilders during this period is arresting.

What accounts for the comparative failure of British producers to achieve the increases in tonnage throughput that would have allowed them to invest profitably in higher throughput technology after World War II? While the piecemeal process of technical modernization undertaken in Britain prior to 1955 was followed by a more wholesale restructuring after that date, it is evident that the extent of modernization remained significantly below that in the most competitive yards abroad (Parkinson 1960: 123–5; Patton Report 1962; Booz-Allen and Hamilton Report 1973: 145–58).

The comparatively piecemeal investment policy of most British producers during the early 1950s can best be explained by their satisfactory competitive performance during this period and by their uncertainty over future market conditions. After World War II Britain benefited from a temporary monopoly position in the world market. Much of German, Dutch, and French capacity had been damaged during the war, and the Germans had been forced to surrender equipment under the terms of the peace-treaty. Further, until 1949 restrictions were placed on the size of vessels produced in Germany and Japan, precluding these countries from competing for the ocean-going segment of the market. As a result, Britain was well placed to supply much of world reconstruction demand as well as the expanding demand for tankers. Britain produced 53 per cent of gross tonnage launched in the world during the period 1946–7, and 43 per cent between 1948 and 1950. Britain's share of the export market between 1948 and 1950 was 35 per cent. While British producers were progressively outcompeted in the export market after 1951, their secure position in the home market prior to 1955 continued to assure them full order books and high profitability.[14]

Given their secure position in the home market and their high profitability during this period, it is not surprising that British producers continued to opt for comparatively labour-intensive methods. Historically, as we have seen, British producers used labour-intensive techniques as compared with German and especially American producers who, responding to shortages of

[14] See Tables 4.1 and 4.2. According to an industrial financial report prepared by *The Economist* for the SEF in Feb. 1954, industry profitability was high at this time. Between the first quarter of 1949 and the first quarter of 1953, the net worth of twenty-one quoted companies increased from £45.8 million to £69.8 million. Profits, net of taxes and other charges but including depreciation allowances, were £23.5 million. (Modern Records Centre, University of Warwick, MSS 44/TBN 15, File 3.)

labour or to the high price of labour, invested in more mechanized methods. The use of these comparatively labour-intensive methods allowed British producers to avoid the overheads that often proved crippling to firms abroad during periods of recession, given their large commitments to fixed capital equipment (see Ch. 2).

Further, given the historical volatility of market demand in shipbuilding, it was reasonable that British producers should form cautious expectations of future market demand after the war.[15] As the quote below suggests, British shipbuilders no doubt were concerned that the post-war boom might be followed by bust, much on the pattern of the inter-war period.[16]

If the 'bulls' are right, and the present strength of the freight market develops into what may be described as a 'boom' next year, and if it continues for any length of time, owners will undoubtedly become more interested in the possibility of acquiring additional vessels, whether secondhand or new. A resumption of ordering for dry-cargo ships will be welcomed by the shipyards; but it cannot be expected on any large-scale, at least until the huge volume of war-built tonnage still in existence begins to show definite signs of breaking down or wearing out (the *Shipping World and World Shipbuilding*, 1 Dec. 1954: 581).

The use of comparatively labour-intensive methods was therefore the retention by British shipbuilders, under conditions of market uncertainty, of a traditional formula that had secured their competitive success in the past.

This argument is difficult to sustain for the years 1955–65, characterized first by progressive import penetration and subsequently by declining profitability.[17] The efforts of the British to modernize their facilities after 1955 in emulation of their competitors abroad suggests an acceptance of the superiority of more capital-intensive methods. The comparatively limited extent of technical and organization modernization in Britain during this

---

[15] See Fig. 4.1 for fluctuations in world shipbuilding output between 1890 and 1970.

[16] Also see the *Shipbuilder and Marine Engine Builder* (Aug. 1954: 473); the *Shipping World and World Shipbuilding* (6 Jan. 1954: 1; 3 Mar. 1954: 243; 1 Sep. 1954: 581).

[17] A private survey conducted by Hoare and Co. showed that the industry profit/sales ratio fell from 6.4% in 1958 to 2.4% in 1964. See Slaven (1981a: 21).

TABLE 4.4. Registration of ships launched in selected countries

Country	Average in 000s		%age increase
	1954–6	1964–6	
UK	1,007	1,204	20
Germany	449	446	0
Japan	340	2,194	545
Norway	804	2,076	158
Sweden	220	404	84
France	243	332	37

Source: Lloyd's Register of Shipping, Annual Shipbuilding Returns.

period can be accounted for by considering certain distinctive features of British market structure which constrained British producers from expanding their scale of production.

First of all, certain of Britain's major competitors benefited from faster growing domestic markets in which they enjoyed protected positions stemming from such factors as established ties between owners and builders, geography, and government subsidization (Drewry 1972–3; Jones 1957: 224–5).[18] Table 4.4 shows a particular striking advantage in the rate of growth of home-market demand for Japan, which had emerged as the most competitive producer by the late 1950s. In addition, Swedish shipbuilders were in a privileged position not only at home, but also in the second-fastest growing market shown in the table, that of Norway (Ollson 1981*a*: 7–10).

With its relatively slow growing home market, the only way Britain could have maintained its share of world production would have been progressively to boost its share of the unprotected parts of the export market. However, there is little reason to believe that British firms were in a position to do this after World War II. Unlike the late nineteenth and early twentieth centuries, Britain enjoyed no significant resource-cost advantages or any monopoly over production methods or technology that

[18] Established ties carry such weight in shipbuilding because of the expense and long life of the product. Confidence, once gained, is not easy to lose. Having been lost, it is difficult to regain. See Cairncross and Parkinson (1958: 104).

might have conferred a competitive edge (Parkinson 1960: 198–206).

Given these constraints on market expansion, constraints that were not faced by foreign competitors, British firms had only one way in which they could increase the tonnage throughput of their yards as much as firms abroad: namely, by undergoing a process of structural change. They would have had to close certain yards, and concentrate demand and output in the ones that remained.

The point is clearly illustrated in Table 4.3. As the table shows, though the Swedish industry was small in absolute terms in 1950 compared with the British, the average scale of production of its yards was about the same. Facing rapidly expanding demand, Swedish firms were subsequently able to expand the tonnage produced in their yards without the need for structural transformation.

This raises the question of why some British firms did not take the initiative after 1955 and, by adopting the methods being applied abroad, progressively capture market share from their domestic competitors with a view to benefiting from scale economies. Part of the answer has to do with the imperfectly competitive structure of the shipbuilding industry which made it very difficult to capture market share from competitors. Ships are expensive products and have a long life (averaging some twenty years). Product quality is a major consideration in the decision to purchase, and owners place a high premium on the established reputation of shipbuilders. For these reasons, strong, though frequently informal, ties tended to develop between owners and builders, ties that competitors found difficult to undermine unless they could offer substantial improvements in terms of price and delivery dates (Cairncross and Parkinson 1958: 104).

This latter form of competition was restricted by its large initial investment requirements and the risk of competitive retaliation. Yards built only a few vessels simultaneously. Capturing competitors' market share could not be accomplished on the basis of piecemeal investments in technical modernization which characterized most British firms at this time. Rather, a firm would have to commit substantial resources to expanding its capacity so that competitive delivery dates could be guaranteed. Such investments would be contemplated only if aggressive tendering were reasonably certain to secure a larger share of the market. With one British firm's success implying a large reduction in the sales of domestic competitors, however, the pricing policies of firms could not be regarded as independent. Each firm would have to retaliate if it were to remain in business. The risk to all of such a competitive scramble engendered a live-and-let-live attitude in British shipbuilding which gave customers little to choose from between yards.[19]

In short, with slow growth in demand and a sizeable overhang of outmoded but serviceable capacity, no firm was prepared to take the risk of embarking on a major programme of investment and modernization. Here the distinctive position of British producers should be kept in mind. Swedish and Japanese firms, simply because they faced rapidly expanding demand, were in a position to increase the tonnage throughput of their yards without bearing the risks of a competitive struggle for market share.

That market adjustment can be a slow and ineffective agent for restructuring in imperfectly competitive industries such as ship-building is supported by the history of the French industry, where there was little change prior to the intervention of the state in the 1960s. The French industry, though comparatively small, similarly faced a slow growing home-market demand and had a fragmented structure (see Tables 4.3 and 4.4). Due in part to the impact of government policy, however, the tonnage produced in the yards was increased almost to the same extent as yards in Sweden, and a high degree of inter-yard specialization was achieved.

Yard specialization took place in two stages. During the 1950s high levels of government subsidization assured a rapid growth of demand for merchant construction. This encouraged an initial conversion of the large yards from a concentration on warship or passenger-liner construction towards tankers, bulk-carriers, and multi-deck cargo ships. The smaller yards tended to establish themselves as producers of simple cargo vessels as well as particu-

---

[19] For a general discussion of how limited market horizons may interact with imperfectly competitive market structures to encourage firms to adopt less than minimum efficient scale plants, see Scherer (1975). For a development of these ideas applied to the British steel industry, see Elbaum (1986).

lar types of sophisticated tonnage (*Navires, ports et chantiers, passim; Nouveautés techniques maritimes*, 1964).[20]

During the 1960s the government's restructuring scheme contributed to a further specialization within the larger yards, such as Chantiers de l'Atlantique, pursuing strategies of series production of standard vessels. Specialization among the smaller firms remained as it had been during the 1950s: builders concentrated on particular types of sophisticated tonnage and cargo vessels, and occasionally produced short series of standard vessels for individual owners.[21]

State intervention in British shipbuilding was, by comparison, tardy. It was only after 1965 that a serious effort was made to reform the industry's structure. The government's 1966 Shipbuilding Inquiry Committee Report (Geddes Report) recommended a regrouping of firms to form larger shipbuilding consortia with an annual capacity of 400,000–600,000 tons and comprising four to six specialized yards. The 1967 Shipbuilding Industry Act provided financial backing for the scheme by authorizing direct grants to yards participating in the restructuring. The result was a considerable regrouping of the industry (Geddes Report 1965–6: 91).

The conservative investment policies of British shipbuilders after World War II as compared with their more successful competitors abroad should not be attributed to their blind adherence to traditional routines. Their initial piecemeal approach was reasonable under conditions of market uncertainty. Their subsequent failure can be accounted for by the constraints which a highly fragmented industrial structure and stagnant domestic market imposed on market-led restructuring. This was a point made by industrial economist J. R. Parkinson (1960: 150–2) as early as 1960 in accounting for the comparative lack of product standardization in British shipbuilding:

---

[20] Chantiers de France and La Ciotat were also distinctive for their high degree of specialization in the production of liquid-gas carriers. See Buret (1968); Chardonnet (1971: 410–11); Morreaux (1978: 92).

[21] Even among the smaller producers, there were some striking examples of long series being produced, as e.g. with two 1968 orders by Kuwait for a series of 50 and a series of 52 standard vessels produced by La Rochelle–La Pallice. See *Navires, ports et chantiers* (Jan. 1962).

In the present circumstances it is difficult to see how the distribution of orders can be improved without some changes in the organisation of shipbuilding and shipowning. It is the character of the market more than any other single factor which weights the scales against further specialization in shipbuilding. There is no question that it is more economical to build similar ships today than it was a half a century ago when skilled labour was abundant and ships were largely hand-assembled at the stocks. The prospects of getting a sufficiency of orders are at least as good. Yet it appears unlikely that further specialization and standardization will result unless ship owners and shipbuilders concert their efforts to concentrate demand and production on as limited a range of types and sizes of vessels as is consistent with the real requirements of various trades.... This could not, however, occur without some interference with normal marketing arrangements either by the establishment of some central agency governing the placing of orders amongst shipyards or by outright amalgamation.

Prior to the formation of the Shipbuilding Conference in 1928, the employers lacked the institutional arrangement that might facilitate a co-ordinated restructuring of the industry. This was a weakness identified by the Booth Committee as early as 1918 (Booth Committee 1918: 30–1):

Whilst almost all the important materials used by Shipbuilders and Marine Engineers are controlled at the source of supply, whilst Steamship Companies are consolidating their interests, and whilst individual Trade Unions are strongly organised and federated, there is as yet no effective combination among Shipbuilders and Marine Engineers.

It is true that Federations of Shipbuilders and Engineers exist, but these are principally concerned with wages and conditions of labour.

The tendency of the world appears to be in the direction of larger economic organisations, a tendency manifest in Shipping as in Steelmaking, and, unless analogous steps are taken by Shipbuilders and Marine Engineers to meet the new situation, it is to be feared that the industries may suffer needlessly to the detriment of the nation.

Even after the formation of the Shipbuilding Conference, efforts to restructure the industry invariably depended on outside intervention. During the 1930s reform was promoted by the Bank of England. The support of the Clearing Banks, who had a controlling interest in the industry, was key to gaining general acceptance by builders for the proposed reforms. The result was a reduction in industry capacity but little restructuring of the industry's technological or productive capacity (see Ch. 2).

After 1965, with industrial collapse imminent, restructuring was actively supported by the state under the terms of the 1967 Shipbuilding Industry Act. The result of these efforts was an increase in average throughput per yard and a significant tendency towards inter-yard specialization.

Austin and Pickersgill emerged as the most highly specialized of the firms, adopting a strategy in 1968 of producing series of standard 14,500-tons Liberty replacement cargo vessels. Seventy-seven of these were produced between 1970 and 1979. Govan Shipbuilders after its formation in 1972 adopted a similar strategy but with less success. Cammell Laird also adopted this strategy after being brought into public ownership in 1972, but its design never achieved any notable success. Doxford and Sunderland came to approximate most closely the vision of specialization envisaged in the Geddes Report. The firm's Deptford and North Sands yards were adapted for bulk-carrier production while the reconstructed Pallion facility was used for medium-sized general cargo ships. Both Scott-Lithgow and Harland and Wolff began to reconstruct their facilities for VLCC production, but both proved victim of the unanticipated rise in oil prices and collapse of the tanker market after 1974 (Stopford 1979).

The restructuring of British shipbuilding occurred too late. Its impact was just being felt when the post-1975 recession and increasing uncertainty in world shipbuilding markets made it more difficult for firms to consolidate mass markets. As shown in Table 4.5, both Britain and its principal European competitors sustained striking declines in their absolute levels of shipbuilding output after 1975.

European producers are now showing a distinct preference for less capital-intensive and more flexible methods than those characteristic of the 1950s and 1960s. It may well be argued that these conditions are temporary, and that some future recovery will again place the competitive advantage with large specialized yards producing standard vessels in series. But the rapid rise of shipbuilding in South Korea and Taiwan shown in Table 4.5 speaks poorly for ability of builders in Britain, or any other comparatively high-wage country, successfully to pursue a

TABLE 4.5. Shipbuilding output in selected countries, 1975–87

Country	Tonnage launched in million of gross tons				%age change
	1975	1980	1985	1987	1975–87
UK	1.30	0.24	0.14	0.05	−96
France	1.30	0.33	0.19	0.20	−85
W. Germany	2.55	0.46	0.63	0.22	−91
Sweden	2.46	0.34	0.21	n/a	n/a
Japan	17.99	7.29	9.30	4.17	−77
Korea	0.46	0.63	2.78	2.30	+400
Taiwan	0.14	0.29	0.36	0.30	+114

Source: Lloyd's Register of Shipping, Statistical Tables.

strategy of standardization, given the ease with which a work-force can be trained to produce these comparatively simple vessels.

In a manner parallel to the pre-World War II period, it may well be the case that the success of European nations in ship-building will depend on their ability to diversify the product range of their industries, seek specialty markets, and develop the processes to do this efficiently. Ironically, the present challenge facing British shipbuilders may be that of regaining some of their former flexibility and diversity.

While it is uncertain whether large-scale specialized facilities will prove a future advantage or handicap for European ship-builders, this quandary does not detract from the validity of the analysis presented in this chapter. In contrast to the current period, during which all European shipbuilding nations have sustained absolute declines, the British decline of the 1950s and 1960s stands out as distinct. A partial explanation for this is the failure of British builders to benefit from the economies associated with investing in high throughput technology suitable for the expanding mass markets of that era.

Chapter 5 addresses a further part of the explanation for British decline during the 1950s and 1960s. British shipbuilders failed to adopt the bureaucratic methods of work administration that

were successfully used abroad during this period. While the pecu-
liarities of British industry structure discussed in this chapter no
doubt increased management's uncertainty concerning the suitability of bureaucratic methods, I argue that the ultimate constraint was not the market. The failure to transform methods of
work administration in British shipbuilding resulted from a lack
of trust between labour and management, which frustrated co-
operation around proposed institutional reforms.

5

Enterprise Organization and Competitive Decline, 1948–1970

THE British shipbuilding industry's development after World War II is striking, not only because producers modernized their facilities in a piecemeal manner, but also because they retained traditional methods of enterprise organization. The 1962 Patton Report on shipbuilding technology noted the undeveloped nature of managerial hierarchies in the industry (Patton Report 1962: 75):

The British shipbuilding industry has a long tradition of working with a minimum managerial and technical staff and requires to learn how to effectively integrate and use specialist functions in its management structure, so that real advantage commensurate with the increase in overhead costs is obtained.

A 1973 report commissioned by the Department of Trade and Industry confirmed the continuing rudimentary nature of planning techniques in British shipbuilding, noting the key role of skilled workers and their supervisors (Booz-Allen and Hamilton Report 1973: 143–4):

Except in yards building warships, control of quality and dimensional accuracy is provided by the workforce ... Informal scheduling and planning, depending on the skill and experience at foreman level, is often the only detailed planning available once original plans have been bypassed and due dates have been missed.

The figures in Table 5.1, based on employment returns for the British and French shipbuilding industries, provide further evidence of British builders' use of comparatively skilled labour-intensive methods. As the figures in the table show, the relatively small proportion of staff workers in the British shipbuilding

TABLE 5.1. Staff workers as a %age of the total work-force in Britain and France

	Managerial	Design and Technical	Supervisory	Other[a]	Total
Britain					
1951[b]	1.2	2.2	2.9	4.6	10.9
1966	3.6	3.9	n/a	7.5	n/a
1975	3.0	5.9	3.6	8.6	21.1
France					
1949	1.2	4.9[c]	6.1	9.6	21.8
1962[d]	2.9	9.6	6.2	8.2	27.9
1975	3.0	12.3	8.1	7.2	30.6

[a] 'Other' refers primarily to clerical and office staff.
[b] 1951 figures are for England and Wales only.
[c] Technicians are included under 'Other' for the 1949 French figures.
[d] Includes marine engineering.

Sources: Britain—1951: Census of Population for England and Wales; 1966 and 1975: *Department of Employment Gazette.*
France—1949: Latty (1951: 268); 1962: INSEE (1963); 1975: Commissariat générale du plan (1976).

industry cannot be accounted for by significant variations in the proportion of managerial, clerical, or secretarial staff employed in the two countries, but rather by differences in the proportion of designers, technicians, and supervisors. The comparatively small proportion of supervisors in British shipbuilding is especially striking. These differences are consistent with the observation that British workers exercised considerable autonomy in the production process and that there was comparatively little production pre-planning.[1]

The retention of methods of work organization relying critically on the judgement and experience of skilled workers reflected in part a managerial perception that the industry's particular technical and market characteristics precluded the use of more

---

[1] Also see the Patton Report (1962: 25). Of the yards which the committee preparing the report investigated in Germany, Scandinavia, Holland, and Britain, the ratio of workers to foremen was the highest in the British yards.

systematic methods of production planning (Comments of W. Jobbling, technical director of W. Doxford and Sons, in Orenstein 1944–5: D62):

My mind goes back a year or two ago when I was directly connected with a similar planning scheme which was tried out, but it was found that what could be applied in an engineering shop was not suitable in a shipyard. The scheme did not work very successfully at that time ... I think shipbuilding is an industry which is distinct from any other, and to get improved production in ships the detailed production planning system as applied to engineering is, in my humble opinion, rather out of the question.

According to one influential school of thought on Britain's relative decline, perceptions such as those expressed in the above quote reflected a culturally induced contempt for radical departures from established ways of doing things. British management chose conservatively out of conservatism (Aldcroft 1964; Landes 1969). In this chapter I argue, to the contrary, that there was a basis in rationality (or bounded-rationality) for British conservatism. The failure to change was a reasonable response to market uncertainty and to the lack of trust between labour and management with frustrated efforts to reform enterprise organization.[2]

I. The Firm as Routine and Information Channel

One general explanation for the failure to make adaptations to the initial form of an organization relies on the idea of irreversible investments (Arrow 1974: 35–43). The operation of a complex organization involves an investment of time and resources in establishing specialized information channels. While the value of these channels for acquiring information in the future is uncertain, learning the codes, or ways of conveying information, to make efficient use of the channels is from the individual's point of view an irreversible investment. To the extent that the codes are firm-specific, the investment also is irreversible from the organization's point of view. Consequently, even if subsequent in-

---

[2] See Ch. 1 for a discussion of different modes of explanation in the debate on Britain's relative economic decline.

formation suggests that the original choice of channels is wrong, it will not pay to reverse the decision because the costs of change are the costs of unanticipated obsolescence.

This argument carries little weight in the case of British ship-building because of certain distinctive features of its craft system of organization. The production control system in British ship-building was highly informal, while the costs of learning to oper-ate it were ultimately born by the skilled workers. For the core set of metal-working tasks in hull construction, the British system of craft production relied on the interdependency between and general knowledge of skilled workers who formed squads. These squads worked on the basis of a modification of the internal contract system, being paid so much per row of plates or per set of frames, and being responsible for organizing their less skilled assistants who were paid on a time-basis. In the case of the plating squads, for example, while skilled workers specialized in templating, shearing, bending, or furnacing, each had a working knowledge of the others' responsibilities and tasks and conse-quently could co-ordinate his own work in relation to that of his squad partners without the need for higher level supervision. Broader knowledge was the pre-condition for workable spe-cialization independent of managerial control.[3]

The work-force acquired the necessary skills to co-ordinate the production process through well-developed systems of apprenticeship which were administered by the trade unions. Recruits normally served a five-year apprenticeship throughout which time they were paid considerably below the skilled rate. The fact that skills were for the most part industry- as opposed to firm-specific meant that employers were constrained to recoup their initial investment in training by paying relatively low wages throughout the period of apprentice indenture.[4]

A more plausible explanation for the conservatism of British shipbuilders would start from the observation of A. L. Stinch-combe that different types of organizational structures are suit-able for different market environments (Stinchcombe 1960). In

---

[3] These features of the craft system in British shipbuilding are discussed more fully in Ch. 2.
[4] See Elbaum (1989) and Ch. 3, n. 10.

general, bureaucratization of work administration depends on long-term stability of work-flows. Only under such conditions will the overheads associated with the firm-specific information-processing structures required to operate bureaucratic systems be sufficiently productive to make them economical (Stinchcombe 1959–60; 168–87). The flexible British system of craft production proved to be highly successful during the late nineteenth and early twentieth centuries because of the nature of the market and the technology. The product was non-standard, most skills were industry- as opposed to firm-specific, and firm output levels were variable. The generally trained British workers were easily able to adapt to an ever-changing product mix without the need for upper level supervision. They were also able to move between yards in a district as firm output levels varied (Ch. 2).

After World War II there were a number of significant changes in technology and product-market conditions in world shipbuilding (see Ch. 4). Ships became larger and more standardized. The rapid increase in world demand for ships in combination with a new, more capital-intensive technology based on welding and prefabrication encouraged often dramatic increases in the scale of production. With significant variations between stages of ship-construction, the result was increasing routinization of work and its simplification through mechanization. This in turn facilitated the effective use of scientific management techniques.

Work Routinization and Skills

Generally speaking, the extent to which it has been possible to mechanize production in shipbuilding has been greater at the initial stages of metal fabrication in the sheds than at the latter stages of block assembly at the berth or at the final stage of outfitting the vessel. This follows from the fact that with pre-fabrication of the hull, the aim is to start with relatively simple and standard shaped components which are built up into more complex and larger block assemblies. In constructing a large tanker or bulk-carrier, for example, most of the hull can be built up from standard panels, which consist of a series of three or four steel plates, cut rectangularly, welded together in a row, to which steel beams are welded to stiffen the structure (Boekholt 1971; Cuthbert 1969).

Technically, it has proved relatively easy to mechanize this stage of production, since the surfaces to be burnt or welded are flat and can be placed on a flat surface over which a mechanized burning or welding unit can be set to move in a straight lateral or longitudinal direction.[5] This stage of assembly and welding lent itself readily to an adaptation of mass-production techniques with the development of the 'panel-line' during the 1960s, the ship-building industry's version of Ford's assembly line. The basic panel-line consists of a conveyor belt on which plates (three or four), after being cut rectangular, are clamped magnetically, tacked, and welded, either on one side or with a turnover facility, to be followed by a gantry which automatically positions, clamps, and welds stiffeners (steel beams) to the row of plates (Cuthbert 1969: 123–4, 127–9). The use of the system effectively reduced this stage of assembly and welding to a machine-tending process after the plates and machines were appropriately set.[6]

Of course, not all plates in shipbuilding are burnt to rectangular shape. But even in such cases, as the plate surface is flat and as only two-dimensional burning motion is required, it was relatively easy to construct a mechanized burning unit that could be guided by profiles or templates.[7] An extension of this latter principle from the late 1950s was the development of 1 : 10-scale lofting in conjunction with optically controlled burning machines. In this system, the dimensions of the plates, rather than being

---

[5] See the *Procedure Handbook of Arc Welding* (1973) for a description of the Union Melt automatic welding system.

[6] This assertion should be qualified by noting that not all sections of the hull, even in the case of a large tanker, can be built up from rectangular boxes or panels. The fore and aft section as well as plates and stiffeners at the bilge have to be bent to the appropriate curvature and the work has continued to be done in the traditional manner, plates being bent in the cold state on the basis of full-sized templates with hydraulically or electrically powered bending rolls, and beams being furnaced prior to bending at the blocks. (See Ch. 2.) In the mid-1950s improved cold frame bending machines were introduced which saved on labour and reduced skill requirements as it was not necessary to judge the temperature of the steel or compensate for contraction of the metal upon cooling. (SRNA Archives, Part II, No. 17, File 5007), and Shepheard (1943–4: 165–6).

[7] See the Patton Report (1962: 13–14) for a description of the flame-cutting equipment in use in British yards during the 1950s.

developed by loftsmen in full-scale drawings which serve for the production of wooden templates, are developed in 1 : 10-scale drawings.[8] Photostatic plates are then made of the small-scale drawings, which when scanned by an electric eye activate a burning machine (Patton Report 1962: 12–13; Hardy and Tyrrell 1964: 85–6).

It was this early stage of hull construction in yards engaged in the production of vessels in series or specializing in large tankers that came to approximate most nearly the popular conception of deskilled work under conditions of mass production. The tasks of the majority were simplified, routinized, and made increasingly process-specific, while those of the minority involved in design, planning, and machine-setting were upgraded.

This initial stage of assembling and welding plates and beams to form flat panels, however, is only part of the total work involved in constructing the vessel's hull. Panels have to be built up into larger three-dimensional units of varying shape and these have to be transported to the berth and assembled and welded together. The scope for mechanization at these latter stages of hull assembly is limited because of the variety and often awkward locations in which the work has to be carried out. Welding has to be done in the overhead and vertical positions inside prefabricated units, for example, as well as over non-flat surfaces. A problem in mechanizing the welding of connecting floor and deck plating at the berth, is that intervening longitudinal stiffeners or girders hinder the operation of portable mechanized units.

The above features of hull assembly have meant that manual stick welding has remained the predominant form of welding in shipbuilding.[9] Correspondingly, the advantages from series pro-

---

[8] See Ch. 3 for a description of traditional lofting techniques.

[9] Even in the highly mechanized Japanese industry at the end of the 1960s, yards carried out 60 to 70% of their welding with manual processes. See Boekholt (1971: 2) and Cuthbert (1969: 124). The technical knowledge involved in manual stick welding is limited. The correct electrode and amperage has to be selected for the job. High carbon steel used for the vessel's hull, for example, requires a different type of electrode than low carbon steel used for the vessel's interior. The manual dexterity required, though, can be considerable if welding is done overhead or in the vertical position as opposed to the downhand position. Skill requirements are also enhanced for specialized welding techniques such as the TIG (tungsten inert gas) process often used for pipe-work or aluminium work. See Ryan (1977: 9–15).

duction for these stages have derived from the specialization and routinization of essentially manually dependent work it has allowed. These advantages could be quite considerable for the intermediate stage of building up prefabricated units from panels, where an assembly-line concept of work could be applied, the worker and machine remaining at one work station while the materials flowed past. At the final stage of assembly at the berth, however, the possibilities for routinizing the work were diminished, as the worker had to move over the vessel to work in a variety of locations.

In the case of outfitting the vessel, it is important to distinguish between the fabrication of the components in the sheds and their installation in the vessel's hull. For the installation of electrical fittings, pipes, wooden fixtures, etc., similar considerations apply to those discussed for the latter stages of hull assembly. The work is carried out in a variety of awkward locations, which has limited the scope for mechanizing or routinizing the work. In the case of the fabrication of components, there have been certain technical developments which have arguably decreased the inherent skill requirements for the work of certain trades. Blacksmiths, for example, were traditionally responsible for forging a variety of small ship's fittings such as flange connections for pipes, door-hinges, and deck-mountings. They also forged such large structural items as the stem and stern-frame which might alternatively be casted by iron-moulders.[10] The work of the smith was labour-intensive and often required a high degree of skill and experience as L. T. C. Rolt's (1971: 96) description below suggests:

the making of heavy forgings called for perfect coordination between the master smith, who was in charge of the operation, his hammer drivers who stood behind the hammer and worked the steam valve handle which caused the hammer to strike a hard or soft blow, and the men who clinging to the long chain-supported tongs, manipulated the glowing billet on the anvil as the smith directed . . . long experience in his craft had given him powers of judgement that seemed almost uncanny.

As early as during World War I, oxy-acetylene welding was introduced for connecting flanges to pipes. Drop-hammer forging,

---

[10] See Smellie (1923: 92–100) for a description of the work traditionally carried out by smiths and moulders.

a relatively unskilled process, was also introduced at this time to produce a variety of small fittings and components when repeat work was possible (Tuckett 1974: 211–16). The more significant advances, though, came during World War II with the introduction of arc welding and burning for fabricating large structural items such as the stern-frame and rubber-post which formerly had been forged or casted (Redshaw 1949: 38^r). A variety of simple casting techniques were also introduced at this time, such as gravity-die casting and centrifugal casting for cylindrical shapes (Fyrth and Collins 1959: 245–6).

Welding and burning also transformed the work of sheet-plate-workers who worked with the thinner varieties of tin and steel plate. The effect on skill requirements was similar to that for more heavy plating work. Profile-burning machines were introduced during the 1940s to cut sections to shape, while welding replaced traditional joining techniques. Generally spot welding, a form of resistance welding, has been used on this work rather than the arc process. In this technique, the welding cycle is entirely automatic after the components have been correctly positioned.[11]

While technical change has arguably decreased the inherent skill requirements for producing many ship's fittings, the work nevertheless has generally tended to lack the routinized quality of the early stages of hull assembly. This is because even when successive hulls built by a yard for various owners are standard, outfitting specifications are apt to vary, which has lessened the scope for repeat work. This has encouraged firms to retain the traditional practice of relying on the work-force to lift the templates and specifications they need to produce many components directly from the vessel's hull, possibly with the guidance of general arrangement drawings. Correspondingly, the work has tended to retain more of its traditional craft character.

From the above description of the development of shipyard technology and methods of construction after World War II, a

---

[11] In resistance welding a high current of low voltage is passed through the components to be joined by means of a high conductivity electrode. Heat is generated at the interface where the components touch and the surfaces melt and fuse to form a weld nugget. In spot welding, the sheet metals are lapped and clamped together between cylindrical copper-alloy electrodes making a series of spot welds at discrete intervals.

number of points should be emphasized for the discussion which follows. First, as regards the general nature of the technology, there are certain continuities and certain changes with the past. The industry has continued to build a large and complex product requiring the use of a range of techniques. The extent to which these techniques have been susceptible to mechanization and routinization, however, has varied. For the latter stages of hull assembly at the berth, as well as for the process of installing fittings in the completed hull, the differences with the past would appear to be more of degree than kind. Regardless of how standard output is, the work has continued to be labour-intensive in character and carried out in a variety of locations.

For the earlier stages of hull construction, the introduction of welding and prefabrication opened up the possibility for changes more qualitative in nature. At the earlier stages the worker can potentially be tied to one location in the flow of production while the materials move past. Further, if output is fairly specialized and component production is standardized, a division of labour can be established which is not too dissimilar from that envisaged by Adam Smith in his famous example of pin manufacture. The worker can repeatedly perform one type of operation at one point in the flow of production.

The emergence of this simplified division of labour during the 1950s and 1960s in yards producing standard ships in series or specializing in supertanker production facilitated the effective use of more systematic planning techniques. Evidence that progress in the use of such techniques depended critically on the degree of product standardization is provided by the comparative experience of French and Swedish shipbuilding. A 1953 internal memo of the Ateliers et Chantiers de Provence, reporting on the yard's investigatory mission to the Kochums yard in Sweden, noted the following (Archives des ateliers et chantiers de Provence, 1953):[12]

---

[12] L. Oury's autobiographical account of his years at the Chantiers de l'Atlantique in Saint-Nazaire during the 1950s indicates that the yard was experiencing the same sort of problems in planning that were experienced during the inter-war period (see above, Ch. 2). In his description of the payment-by-results system employed at the yard, Oury notes that the allocated times for jobs were often determined in an *ad hoc* manner and that jobs were often initiated before an allocated time had been determined for them. See Oury (1973: 73–9).

The high degree of success observed [at Kochums] in reducing 'lost time' (both disastrous for the firm and a loss of income for the workforce) is due to the organization and the preparation of the work . . . to a complete definition of the work in advance.

When we attempt to use the methods of K. here, we come to appreciate that our situation is poorly adapted to it because it is necessary first to satisfy certain conditions . . . In a word, while K. produces vessels in mass that they have designed or are familiar with, we only produce vessels in units, whose projects and studies do not depend solely on us. What K. achieves easily in preparing a plan is not possible here, or at least cannot be guaranteed outside exceptional cases.

In the case of France, as yards became more specialized after 1960, and as series production became more common, the scope for comprehensive production planning increased. However, as A. Ravaille's 1964 description of planning methods at La Ciotat near Marseille indicates, difficulties were still encountered. Ravaille identified three basic obstacles to comprehensive production planning at La Ciotat: the complexity of the product, the shortness of the series of standard vessels produced, and difficulties in gaining advance acceptance for a particular design from the owner (Ravaille 1964: 124–5, 136). The yard responded to the latter problem by preparing an approximate and flexible plan, the details of which could be completed as production progressed.

The highly specialized Swedish shipyards were among the most successful in using systematic planning methods after World War II. The considerable success in employing these techniques at the Eriksberg yard in Gothenburg is described in a 1961 report of a French investigatory mission (*Navires, ports et chantiers*, Jan. 1962: 13):

The study they made allowed the yard [Eriksberg] to determine that 60 per cent of their expenditure (value added) in building a ship corresponded to transporting personnel and materials and only 40 per cent to work on constructing the vessel *per se*. Consequently they decided to rationalize the transportation system and to minimize the movements of the personnel by keeping a worker at the same work station and by assuring that the same team always would do the same work at the same point. But, a highly developed planning system is needed to achieve this and the work plan has to be established very carefully in advance.

Given British shipbuilders' long history of competitive success based on the craft system of production, their reluctance to jettison it and embrace bureaucratic methods of work administration during the 1950s is perhaps understandable. British shipbuilders had experienced periodic and severe depressions in demand and output in the past. Management no doubt was uncertain whether the rapid expansion of the 1950s would continue into the 1960s, or be followed by a collapse that would shift the competitive advantage back towards the informal production system they currently were using (Parkinson 1956: 244–5):[13]

United Kingdom shipbuilders may feel that the present rate of output corresponds closely to the level of orders that is likely to be forthcoming on the average during periods of, say, five or more years, and that the long-term prospect of keeping the industry fully employed at all times does not justify the costly effort that would be needed to expand output rapidly over the next few years. There is much to be said for this view, but it cannot be accepted without question.

A larger shipbuilding output in the United Kingdom would mean, of course, that more would be at stake if orders became hard to get . . . But the shipbuilding industry cannot expect to escape unscathed from the vicissitudes of world trade and sea transport, and, in spite of ten years of maximum output cushioned by a long order book, it must be prepared in the long run to adjust its output and its prices, as well as its order book, to fluctuations in demand . . . it must be ready to cash in on the boom as well as to prepare for a slump, and it is with this in mind that concern may be felt about the slow expansion of United Kingdom shipbuilding output.

For this to be a plausible interpretation, we must explain why producers abroad acted differently. Why did Britain's competitors respond to market uncertainty differently and decide to pin their hopes on the application of systematic planning methods? The answer is they did not. There was an important element of luck in the successful use of systematic management techniques by producers abroad. Swedish and French builders, for example, did not react differently to market conditions and decide to adopt bureaucratic methods after World War II. These producers,

[13] For evidence from the trade journals, refer to the citations in Ch. 4, n. 15. For the comparative stability of shipbuilding output after World War II, see Fig. 4.1.

much as the British, continued to do what they had always done. Conservatism was pervasive.

From the first years of the twentieth century onwards there is evidence of significant differences in the methods of planning and work administration used by British and foreign shipbuilders (see Ch. 3). Product-market conditions at this time bestowed the competitive advantage on the flexible craft system of production which relies on the expertise of manual workers. Britain consequently benefited from its ample supplies of skilled labour concentrated in shipbuilding districts. Producers abroad, facing shortages of skilled labour, were constrained to establish bureaucratic systems of work administration suitable for a less well-trained work-force. This connection between conditions of labour supply and methods of work administration was observed by industrial economist J. R. Parkinson as early as 1956:

Yet the impression remains that Continental shipbuilders were anticipating [during the 1930s] the changes which would take place in shipyard organisation in the next ten or twenty years rather more readily than shipbuilders in the United Kingdom.

Paradoxically the Continental shipbuilders were drawing ahead because they did not dispose of adequate supplies of skilled labour. The legacy of skill in the British shipyards made it possible to build ships with the minimum of planning and labour supervision...The shortage of skilled labour on the Continent made such methods impracticable, and they were abandoned in favour of preparing detailed plans in the drawing office and templates in the loft, which could be used by semi-skilled labour in the marking and processing of material (Parkinson 1956: 237).

Both British and foreign builders continued to do what they always had done after World War II. Foreign producers experienced unanticipated benefits from a system that labour-market constraints had compelled them to adopt in the past. British builders, in an unanticipated manner, witnessed their fortunes decline.

This analysis suggests an evolutionary explanation of outcomes in the shipbuilding industry along the lines of Nelson and Winter's (1982) work, in which *ex ante* blindness and luck combined with *ex post* market-selection forces to determine which firms are successful. While on the face of it there is much to commend this interpretation, I shall argue, while luck played a role, constraints were also important in determining outcomes. The opportunities of British shipbuilders were narrowed by the lack of *trust* between labour and management, which frustrated co-operative efforts to reform the industry's institutional structure. To develop this argument I now turn to the idea of enterprise organization as compromise.

II. The Firm as Compromise

The competitive success of British shipbuilders based on the craft system of organization suggests an understanding of the system as a set of institutions that were retained because of their efficiency properties and the mutual benefits they generated for skilled workers and their employers. While the craft system undoubtedly had advantages over more formal and bureaucratic systems and produced joint benefits, this did not preclude conflict between the principal actors. Not only were there serious differences between the employers and skilled workers over questions of machine manning, but there were also disputes among competing groups of skilled workers over the allocation of work. This suggests that the craft system in British shipbuilding, rather than an equilibrium solution to the problem of finding the most efficient way to organize production, should be seen as a compromise, where each actor recognized that the others had an interest in sustaining the system, but also an interest in shifting the terms of the agreement to their own advantage.

The relevance of the notion of compromise to the failure to reform the British system of work administration can be illustrated by considering the manner in which welding technology was substituted for the traditional method of hull construction based on riveting. Although welding only came to be generally applied in Britain after World War II, its organization was determined by the outcome of a series of conflicts during the 1930s and early 1940s when it was first introduced.[14]

---

[14] The following discussion of the events surrounding the introduction of welding is based on Lorenz (1981). For a related discussion of these events, drawing on the same archive sources, see McGoldrick (1982: 168–80).

During the 1930s welding was initially used as a supplement to riveting on main structural work in ship-hull construction. The technology at this stage in Britain was almost entirely confined to the principal warship contractors such as Vickers-Armstrong; Cammell Laird; Swan, Hunter and Wigham Richardson; and John Brown. Despite this limited extent of practical applications, by the 1930s the view was widespread among British shipbuilders that the all-welded hull would eventually make traditional riveted construction obsolete.[15]

It was in this context of limited practical experience, but with an eye to the future, that employers in the British industry set up during the early 1930s a committee to establish a national policy for manning and rates on welding. This reflected their concern that, in the absence of a national policy, the division of labour and rates on welding would be introduced in an *ad hoc* manner at the yard level, the result of innumerable conflicts between employers and groups of skilled workers. Past experience argued that the outcome of such fragmented conflicts could well be to the advantage of strategically placed groups of skilled workers who, backed by wider union organizations, would be able to impose their terms.

There were already a number of disconcerting bits of evidence. Those naval contractors who had applied the technique to any great extent were paying exceedingly high time rates. Cammell Laird at Birkenhead, for example, was paying members of the Boilermakers' Society a rate of 80s. to 90s. per week, substantially above the national uniform rate for skilled trades of 60s. negotiated in 1929. J. Samuel White, while engaged on an Admiralty contract for a cruiser, had unsuccessfully tried to apply the caulker's plain time-rate of 57s 6d. per week and instead was paying 74s. 6d. to caulker members of the Boilermakers' Society (SRNA Archives, London Minute Books, 24 Feb. and 28 May 1931). Further, with attempts by the Boilermakers' Society during the early 1930s to establish proprietary rights to welding, competing claims for the right to use welding plant had been filed with the SEF by the Blacksmiths' Society, the Plumbers' Associa-

[15] SRNA Archives, Federation Circulars, 9 Jan. and 28 Sept. 1932.

tion and the SSA (SRNA Archives, London Minute Books, 16 July, 28–29 Jan., and 21–25 Feb. 1932). Employers faced both the prospect of costly demarcation disputes and the real possibility, that in the absence of a nationally coordinated employer policy, the well-organized Boilermakers' Society would establish exclusive rights to welding at a rate some 20 to 30 per cent above the national uniform rate.

As early as 1931 the SEF set up a committee to consider rates and conditions applicable to all welding work, both on hull construction and outfitting. Based on the committee's deliberations, the SEF presented its welding scheme to the unions in general conference in July of 1932. The scheme called for the creation of a new class of skilled workers, ship-welders, to be organized and trained outside the existing union structure and to be recruited initially from the supply of shipyard workers and apprentices, but not necessarily from those displaced by the process. The allocation of welding between ship-welders and other trades was to be at the discretion of the employer. Remuneration was to be at the national uniform rate for skilled labour, 60*s*. per week. Trainees with prior shipyard experience, whether skilled, semi-skilled, or unskilled, were to undergo a two-year training period and to start at the rate of 41*s*. per week and advance to 60*s*. by equal half-yearly instalments. In the case of semi- and unskilled workers, progression to the 60*s*. was to be dependent on the employer's assessment of progress (McGoldrick 1982: 168–80; SRNA Archives, Federation Circulars, 7 Mar. 1933).

The SEF's welding scheme was hardly revolutionary in nature. Its essentially conservative nature can be highlighted by contrasting it with a set of proposals in a March 1933 committee report calling for the elimination of the squad contract system of organization (SRNA Archives, Federation Circulars, on Mar. 1933). The report specified the following: (1) that plate straightening could be done by unskilled platers' helpers; (2) that there was no general need for platers in attendance during plate mangling; (3) that plate and angle-iron shearing could be done by semi-skilled workers, as it required no special skills; (4) that it might be advisable to sectionalize platers' work, restricting platers to their sheds and making erection at the bay the responsibility of semi-skilled 'erectors'; and (5) that general care should be taken not to pay the skilled rate on new machine operations that could be done by less skilled men at lower rates.

The proposals were based in most details on the practices of one unnamed firm with extensive experience with welding (SRNA Archives, Federation Circulars, 28 Nov. 1932):

the squad system had been dispensed with, individual platers with necessary help employed on the operations of mangling and flanging. The work of planning continued to be carried out by a semi-skilled man. At the welding tables the plates were set in position by the welder after which any lining off was done by the loftsman. The shaping and cutting of the plates and bars was then done by a semi-skilled man using an oxyhydrogen cutting machine, which machine was capable of cutting 100 feet per hour. As regards the erection of the work on the ship it was explained that the firm were following the previous system of employing yard labourers to transport the work to the ship where it was erected in position by a framing squad.

The firm's practice amounted to a break-up of the squad contract system, with platers being confined to the more skilled fabrication tasks in the sheds: bending, flanging, joggling, and furnacing. Loftsmen laid off the work instead of platers, indicating a switch to the pre-templating system, while labourers were responsible for transporting the material to the stocks.[16] These practices, if applied more generally in Britain, would have resulted in an increase in the detailed division of labour and a substitution of cheaper non-apprenticed labour for skilled labour on the more simple jobs. They consequently would have required establishing a more bureaucratic system of production control to replace the non-bureaucratic one provided by the squads.

The dilution proposals almost certainly reflected the interests of the minority of naval contractors within the employers' federation. First, naval producers were the only firms with considerable experience with welding by the early 1930s. Secondly, such major warship specialists such as Vickers-Armstrong, Cammel Laird, and John Brown were large vertically integrated firms, with interests in steel, munitions, and possibly heavy engineering. The

---

[16] For a discussion of lofting techniques and their relation to the use of more systematic planning methods, see Ch. 3.

wartime experience of these firms as mass producers of munitions had provided them with a model of more systematically organized production. Drawing on this experience, it is not unreasonable that these firms should look for ways to apply these organizational lessons to shipbuilding.

Naval contractors also had to meet fairly strict requirements if they hoped to be placed on the select list of firms from which the Admiralty requested tenders. These requirements bore not only upon the quality of equipment and technical capabilities of the yard, but also upon its methods of organization and control, which the Admiralty saw as bearing directly on the quality of workmanship. Confirmation for the importance of this can be derived from a 1912 dispute between the Admiralty and the warship contractors over the use of the squad contract system. The Admiralty argued that this form of payment was not in keeping with a contract clause requiring private contractors to maintain proper wage books and time-sheets showing the exact wage paid and the time worked by individual workers. This is precisely the sort of information which would allow a firm to assess individual performance (SRNA Archives, Federation Circulars, 2 Oct. 1912).

Evidence for the continuing importance of Admiralty contract requirements for managerial methods into the post-World-War-II era is provided by a report on the shipbuilding industry commissioned by the Department of Trade in 1972 (Booz-Allen and Hamilton Report 1973: 143–4):

The lack of sophistication in the planning system used in most yards does not allow for automatic progress assessment . . . The quality of planning is higher among warshipbuilders, primarily as a result of MOD (N) contract requirements. MOD (N) construction contracts require certain standards of planning for which cost allowances are made and which vary between different types of vessels.

The SEF committee on welding rejected the more radical dilution proposals in 1933. This rejection is consistent with the argument that the less technically sophisticated merchant-builders, who formed the majority of the SEF, believed that the particular technical and market conditions of their industry precluded the effective use of systematic planning techniques.

While the SEF's welding scheme was essentially conservative, it did challenge the established truce between management and labour in an important respect. It called for the training of a new class of skilled ship-welders outside the existing union structure and stipulated that those workers and their unions displaced by welding should not necessarily be the ones to control the new technology.

The unions rejected these proposed changes in general conference in July and November of 1933, and the employers tried to unilaterally introduce them in 1934. The control which the employers sought to exercise over apprenticeship was simply viewed as a thinly veiled opportunistic ploy designed to indirectly dilute with cheaper apprentice labour.[17] The lack of *trust* is apparent in the following remarks made at the November 1933 conference by the vice-president of the SEF and the representative of the NUGMW respectively:

I submit that the proposals in connection with the payment of trainees are in no sense unfair, and the term 'dilution' has no proper use in connection with what is actually happening . . . The suggestion apparently is that although these men are not experts, although they cannot pretend to be experts, it is wrong to pay them less than the 60/- rate while they are being trained.

I am a practical man with 30 years experience in handling these problems, and my colleagues may have more experience but it is the general experience in industry that the lower rate becomes the maximum rate. You may have these men deemed to be failures for the first 12 months or the first 18 months, and out you go and in comes a cheaper man. You may have a few £3 men at the top and a greater proportion of 41/- or 45/- or 50/- men making up the bulk of the men engaged in welding (TUC Library, Shipbuilding File, 1933).

The decision to create a trade outside the existing unions raised the problem of competitive demarcation struggles to lay claim to the new process. An eventual substitution of welding and gas-burning for traditional methods promised to displace the riveting

[17] The unions arguably were predisposed to distrust management's proposals because of the historical legacy of conflict in the industry concerning the employers' right to use cheaper apprentice labour. For disputes over the use of apprentices at the turn of the century during the introduction of pneumatic machinery, see Lorenz (1984: 618–21).

and caulking sections and about 50 per cent of the platers of the Boilermakers' Society. The SSA stood to lose most of their drilling section. Blacksmiths, plumbers, engineers, and coppersmiths had become increasingly dependent on welding and burning in their work.

The executives of the unions met in February 1934 to consider a collective response to the SEF scheme. It was agreed that (SSA Executive Committee Report, 17 Apr. 1934)[18]

the unions here represented pledge themselves to secure that the work to be welded should be done by the class hitherto doing the work. In the event of any member refusing to do the work of another trade being subject to discrimination by the Employers, all Unions here represented pledge themselves to render support to such member in the fullest sense.

On 27 March it was agreed (SSA Executive Committee Report, 27 Mar. 1934)

That in the opinion of the Committee district action is likely to be the most successful, and where the introduction of trainees, or wage reductions, is resisted by members of any Union, they shall receive the fullest support from other Unions in their refusal to do the work under dispute.

These agreements were not successfully implemented. In a manner consistent with their sectional past, the unions pursued isolated competitive strategies. In April 1934 members of the Boilermakers' Society went on strike in opposition to the scheme without support from the other unions in the Tyne, Clyde, and south coast districts. These strikes were resolved when the firms involved, which were mainly naval contractors, agreed to pay the men on a piecework basis in violation of the provisions of the welding scheme (McGoldrick 1982: 178–9; SRNA Archives, Federation Circulars, 28 May 1934).

With employer unity broken the welding scheme in disarray, the allocation of welding work in the yard was determined through a process of competitive struggles between groups of skilled workers and their unions for control of the new process.

---

[18] The unions attending the Feb. and Mar. 1934 meetings were: the Boilermakers, Blacksmiths, Shipwrights, Sheet-Metal-Workers, Engineers, Patternmakers, Plumbers, Electrical Trades, Woodworkers, Painters, and Transport and General Workers.

On a number of occasions the SSA complained that members of its drilling section, who had been retrained for welding work, were being poached by the Boilermakers' Society (SSA Executive Committee Reports, 31 Jan. and 14 June 1933, 6 June and 25 July 1934). For a short period, it appears that the Transport and General Workers' Union successfully recruited welders in the Belfast region (SSA Executive Committee Report, 25 July 1934). By the early 1940s, though, the Boilermakers' Society in large measure had been successful in establishing exclusive rights to arc welding in hull construction. In 1944 the SSA effectively conceded the claim, noting that given the Boilermakers established piece rates on welding and their uncompromising position, it would be unwise to press the issue and alternative sources of employment for displaced drillers were being considered (SSA Executive Committee Report, 23 Mar. 1944). Ship-welders were effectively a new section of the Boilermakers' Society.[19]

The introduction of the related technology of automatic burning machinery presents some similarities as well as significant differences with the case of welding. The potential for dilution on this technology is arguably greater than with welding equipment. Once set, these machines can automatically cut plates or sections to shape and there is little justification for using skilled labour on them. When they were first extensively introduced during World War II in substitution for shearing machines, most firms conceded the right of members of the Boilermakers' Society, who were organized in squads, to operate them. A few firms, led by Vickers-Armstrong, and with SEF backing, attempted to dilute with unskilled labour (SRNA Archives, Part II, No. 17, File 5007).

---

[19] In contrast to main structural work, where members of the Boilermakers were able to pursue a national policy with a great deal of success, the allocation of welding work between Boilermakers and the outfitting trades was much more highly contested. Most of the relevant trades had secured the right to use welding plants within their shops, though there were certain exceptions. At the Clarendon yard on the Scottish east coast, ship-welders carried out welding in the smithy against the protests of the Blacksmiths' Society. At Barclay Curle on the Clyde, ship-welders secured control of welding in the plumbers' shop. The principle area of contention, though, was welding on board the vessel. Here disputes continued to occur well into the 1960s. SRNA Archives, Federation Circulars, 2 Nov. 1948, and Part II, No. 17, File 3918.

The conditions in which this conflict took place were quite different from those in which welding was introduced in the 1930s. Labour-markets were tight and this arguably increased the bargaining power of skilled workers. There is also evidence that the Ministry of Labour put pressure on the SEF to concede on the union's claim so as to avoid any major dispute that might jeopardize the state's naval construction programme (SRNA Archives, Part II, No. 17, File 5007). Despite this, Vickers-Armstrong only conceded the issue in 1949 in the face of the Boilermakers' Society's continued intransigence and a lack of general support by the other firms in the industry. As with the introduction of welding, the position of the skilled workers remained intact.

In other cases, where the question was one of the allocation of work between skilled workers as opposed to dilution, the balance of power between competing groups of skilled workers, backed by their unions, played an important role in determining outcomes. The most notable example during the 1950s was the division of hull-assembly work between plater members of the Boilermakers' Society and metal-working shipwrights, as the extension of prefabrication techniques disrupted the established balance. Prefabrication resulted in a shift of assembly work from the berths to the plating sheds and assembly bays where the Boilermakers' Society maintained a closed shop. The SSA argued on this basis that the existing division of labour between platers and shipwrights at the berth should be adjusted in their favour to compensate for their loss. The claim was rejected by the Boilermakers' Society and the issue remained contentious until the early 1960s, when the merger of the two unions set the stage for a resolution.[20]

It was only during the second half of the 1960s that significant changes were made to methods of work organization in the industry. At this time, management negotiated at the local level a series of productivity agreements offering workers greater job security in exchange for eliminating restrictive demarcation practices. These precedent-setting agreements, however, were only

[20] On the Clyde, the yard most seriously effected by this dispute was A. Stephens and Sons. See McGoldrick (1983: 20–1). For general discussions of demarcation conflicts in the shipbuilding industry during this period, see Brown *et al.* (1972); Eldridge (1968: 91–125); Roberts (1967); Wilkinson (1973).

negotiated following the failure to introduce reforms through collective bargaining at the national level.

III. Institutional Reform

In 1959 initial discussions took place within the SEF concerning a comprehensive reform of existing working practices in order to improve productivity. These discussions resulted in the 1962 plan which the employers presented to the unions in general conference at the national level. Although union opposition led to the breakdown of negotiations and the abandonment of the plan, these discussions were none the less significant in setting the agenda for the more successful local productivity bargaining that took place after 1965 (McGoldrick 1983: 210–11).

The key components of the 1962 scheme were proposals for increased flexibility among the skilled trades and interchangeability of labour, including provisions for upgrading non-apprenticed semi-skilled workers to skilled positions (SRNA Archives, Federation Circulars, 'Scheme for the Reorganization of Labour and Conditions of Employment', Oct. 1962):

> Flexibility . . . means that workers in each group shall be versatile in their employment and shall in the course of their work carry out any work of the group to further their job, using the tools of the group as necessary to do so.
> Interchangeability . . . envisages the transfer of workers from one class of work to another class of work within the same group and between groups as necessary.
> In accordance with the broad principles of flexibility and interchangeability . . . workers shall carry out other work of the group . . . either to progress their own work, or to meet shortages of labour or to obviate temporary unemployment.

Union-imposed restrictions on the flexible allocation of labour had been a source of employer discontent in the British shipbuilding industry from the earliest days of iron and steel construction. The radical change in methods associated with the application of prefabrication techniques from the 1940s increased these concerns. With prefabrication, the ancillary tasks of welding and burning take place at all stages of hull construction. This differs from the prior system of piece-by-piece construction at the berth, where the comparable tasks of riveting and plate-shearing take place primarily at one stage in the process of construction. Consequently, with prefabrication, it was important that platers, blacksmiths, and shipwrights be able to do simple ancillary burning and tack welding to progress their jobs if significant problems of overmanning were to be avoided.

As British firms faced increasingly successful competition in the home market from the late 1950s, restrictions of this sort became less acceptable. J. G. Stephens, director of A. Stephens and Sons, in a speech of 14 November 1957 on demarcation gave some indication of the evident absurdities which arose from the employer's point of view (University of Glasgow Archives, UCS 3/1/186):

> There are innumerable cases in building ships where we have to employ two, three or four different trades to complete one operation which could perfectly well be done by one trade; the loss of time in waiting and staff organisation is enormous . . .
>
> The clearest example perhaps is that of the Tack Welder who stands and watches a plater position a bar. When it is in its place the Tack Welder then tacks it and the Plater stands and watches him, whereas the Plater, or his Helper, could perfectly well do the tack welding. If the Plater and the Shipwright were allowed to do their own tack welding our firm could dispose with 65 men the next day and probably increase the output as well. The same thing can be said for burning, spot welding, drilling and the use of the chipping hammer.

The other key component of the employers' 1962 proposal for organizational reform was increased interchangeability of labour. The issue at stake in seeking greater interchangeability was not preventing overmanning. It was primarily one of responding to immediate shortages of skilled labour which were resulting in serious production bottle-necks. These shortages reached alarming proportions by the second half of the 1960s, as the institutional arrangements that traditionally had secured shipbuilders adequate supplies of trained shipyard labour began to break down.

The Demise of Shipbuilding Industrial Districts

Shortages of skilled labour during the 1960s resulted in part from competition in the labour-market from more successful industries. During the 1950s, while the output of the shipbuilding industry stagnated, such sectors as vehicles, electronics, and chemicals expanded rapidly (Matthews *et al.* 1982: 274–300). By the mid-1960s the traditional dominance of shipbuilding and its connected industries in the regional economies of Clydeside and the north-east coast of England was being progressively undermined (Johnston *et al.* 1971).

State intervention played a role in this process. By protecting certain claims and not others, the state contributed to reshaping regional labour supply. Shortly after the war, the north-east coast of England and Clydeside were designated development areas. New industries were attracted by means of investment incentives and expenditure on infrastructure. Most studies on the impact of the government's regional policy indicate that its effectiveness increased from the early 1960s (Brown 1972: 301–18; Keeble 1976: Ch. 5; Moore and Rhodes 1973: 87–110).

In the Tyne and Wear region, for example, planning proposals just after the war were based on the assumption that the traditional industries in riverside areas (shipbuilding, heavy engineering, and coal) would continue to provide the bulk of the employment, and provisions for housing and infrastructure were made correspondingly (Northern Region Strategy Team Working Paper 1976). By the late 1950s, with the decline in the demand for coal and the beginnings of recession in shipbuilding, the incorrectness of this vision was being recognized. Planning aims were altered towards attracting new industries to the region. During the 1960s new manufacturing employment was primarily attributable to greenfield sites located in the outer belt surrounding the riverside towns. Most of this new employment was in light manufacturing, especially light engineering and mechanical engineering (Northern Region Strategy Team Working Paper 1976: 21–3, 43–50, 72–3).

It was in the context of an absolute decline in shipbuilding output during the 1960s, characterized by sharp fluctuations in output and employment, that the industry sustained a net loss of skilled labour. The SITB made the following report in 1967 for the period from 10 January to 21 May, 1966 (SITB 1966–7: 8):

Out of every 100 skilled workers who left to take up work in another industry, only 85 employees left other industries to enter this industry. The corresponding figures of losses and gains to the industry for apprentices (including pre-apprentices) are 100 and 73. If the two elements of skilled labour force are taken together, the industry's loss of manpower to other industries is 20% over and above its recruitment of labour from those industries.

The continuation of these trends over the following year resulted in an absolute loss of skilled apprentice labour for the 1967–8 period of 10 per cent, while for first-year apprentices alone the figure was closer to 20 per cent. The loss of skilled labour over the period was, as the 1968 SITB report noted, in 'marked contrast to the increase in the volume of training received' (SITB 1967–8: 6, 13).

Skilled apprentices generally benefited from secure indentures in the shipbuilding industry. The loss of this labour to competing sectors is strong support for the view that what was at stake was the pull or attraction of other sectors offering greater long-term security of employment, rather than the push associated with a short-term cyclical down-swing in industry output (Wilkinson 1973: 18–19).

The Content of Reform

Although the 1962 plan was precedent-setting in terms of its scope, there were a number of antecedents in the shipbuilding industry to these negotiations concerning reform of work organization. At the turn of the century the SEF co-ordinated a national effort to negotiate changes in manning arrangements with the introduction of pneumatic machinery (see Ch. 3). They proposed similar negotiations with the unions over manning arrangements on welding technology during the 1930s. In each of these prior cases, national negotiations broke down with the outcome that manning arrangements were determined in an *ad hoc* manner at the yard level. Further, in each case the craft-unions were successful in extending their traditional degree of control over the production process to the new technology.

In this respect the experience of the 1960s is arresting. Starting with the experiment at the Fairfields yard on the Clyde in 1965, a series of productivity agreements were formally negotiated at the local level. Issues which in the past the unions and management had claimed as their unilateral prerogatives were placed on the bargaining table for co-determination.[21]

A number of factors account for the emergence of local productivity bargaining in the shipbuilding industry during the second half of the 1960s. Foremost was the severity of the crisis, as increasingly effective foreign competition forced a number of the major producers to close. The employers identified restrictive union practices as a principal cause of the significant productivity differences between British and Continental producers (Patton Report 1962: 2, 72–3; the *Shipbuilder and Marine Engine Builder*, Apr. 1962: 210; Jan. 1964: 9–10; the *Shipping World and World Shipbuilding*, 6 Jan. 1960; SRNA Archives, Federation Circulars, Oct. 1962). This was an argument which found a degree of acceptance amongst national union officials, who agreed for the first time to allow local productivity bargaining (Wilkinson 1973: 10–13).

Contributing to the change in the attitudes of the union officials at this time were changes in trade-union structure, which altered the occupational boundaries the unions were committed to defending. The most significant structural change was the amalgamation of the Boilermakers' and Blacksmiths' Societies and the SSA, bringing together the large majority of the hull-construction trades in one union, the Amalgamated Society of Boilermakers, Shipwrights, Blacksmiths, and Structural Workers (ASB). From the perspective of the defence of the ASB's occupational base, rigid demarcation lines between the platers and shipwrights or welders and blacksmiths, for example, were no longer necessary. This helps to account for the National Executive's generally positive support for productivity agreements, in so far as relaxation was restricted to ASB member trades (Wilkinson 1973: 22–7).

---

[21] The following discussion of the relaxation of demarcation draws on the unpublished work of Wilkinson (1973). See Alexander and Jenkins (1970) for the history of the Fairfields experiment.

From the perspective of the shop floor and the individual craftsman, the logic of job control as a strategy to protect future job opportunities remained intact. The successful negotiation of relaxation was at once both a question of internal union politics and dependent on individual employers being able to offer a *quid pro quo* (Wilkinson 1973: 20–1).

The question of firms offering a *quid pro quo* brings us to a further point, the importance of the formation of regional multi-yard consortia during the second half of the 1960s and the greater ability of these large firms to offer employment guarantees in exchange for relaxation of restrictive practices. During the 1960s the casual nature of employment in the industry became a focal point of discontent among the workers. As the 1960s progressed, this increasingly resulted in the loss of skilled labour to other sectors offering greater employment security. By operating inter-yard mobility agreements in conjunction with interchangeability between the trades, the multi-yard firms were in a position to offer a greater degree of security of employment than in the past. To this extent, the post-1965 yard amalgamations were a necessary condition for the negotiation of demarcation relaxation.

Finally, it is important to place the relaxation of demarcation practices in the broader national context of a general rise in productivity bargaining in British manufacturing during the 1960s. Inspired in part by the United States' model of plant level bargaining, the view emerged widely amongst employers and government officials that productivity bargaining offered a solution to the distinctively British problem of the growing importance of and lack of formality in plant level bargaining (Donovan Commission 1965–8). The 1960 Fawley productivity agreements are often credited with having set the pace for the agreements that were signed during the first half of the 1960s (Flanders 1964). Between 1966 and 1969 the state provided inspiration and incentive by intending that linking pay increases to productivity was a legitimate way of breaking pay norms and limits.[22]

In the shipbuilding industry, the first experiment in productivity

---

[22] This resulted in a rash of agreements, many apparently quite bogus. Firms were also allowed to break norms if they faced a demonstrable shortage of skilled labour. See Clegg (1979: 141–4, 352–4).

bargaining took place in 1965 under government auspices at the Fairfields yard on the Clyde. However sceptically the Fairfields experiment was viewed at this time by the majority of employers, and however ambiguous the results, it was significant in popularizing the concept of productivity bargaining in ship-building and inspired the numerous company agreements that followed (Alexander and Jenkins 1970; Commission on Industrial Relations 1970–1: 219–37).

How successful was productivity bargaining in the British ship-building industry? This depends on the perspective one is in-terested in. It is clear that relaxation of demarcation marked a significant break with the traditional character of industrial relations and trade-union action in the industry.[23] While results varied from firm to firm, in most cases there was reasonable success in introducing and operating flexibility among the skilled hull-construction trades organized by the ASB. Similarly, inter-yard mobility agreements for these trades were operated with some success (Wilkinson 1973: 22–3). Interchangeability agree-ments were used less, and in particular employers were not successful in upgrading less-skilled non-apprenticed workers to skilled positions.[24]

In the case of the skilled outfitting trades, often organized in competing unions, flexibility and interchangeability were notably less successful. Further, it is clear that the limits of flexibility for the hull-construction trades were precisely the limits of the ASB's occupational boundaries. The ASB was not willing to coun-tenance a break down of demarcation lines between competing craft-unions (Wilkinson 1973: 23–6). Thus, while craft regula-tions were relaxed, trade-union structure set the parameters within which it took place.

While one could conclude on this basis that productivity bar-

---

[23] The path-breaking nature of these agreements can be appreciated by con-sidering that the Boilermakers was not a signatory to the 1912 General Demarca-tion Agreement which contained procedures for resolving demarcation disputes between the unions. The Boilermakers had refused to sign the agreement because it provided for employer representation on the courts charged with arbitrating demarcation conflicts.

[24] See Alexander and Jenkins (1970: 146) on the failure of management to make use of the interchangeability provisions they had bargained for at the Fairfields yard.

gaining was a partial success in the shipbuilding industry, if one considers the issue from the perspective of improvements in labour productivity, the balance sheet is much more ambiguous. Certainly relaxation resulted in no improvements in productivity that helped builders to effectively meet the challenge from foreign competition during the early 1970s (Booz-Allen and Hamilton Report 1973: 154–6).

In this context, it is significant that relaxation of demarcation only constituted a local modification of the traditional craft system of production. Organizational reform did not entail a radical departure in the direction of increased bureaucratization of work administration. The principal actors remained wedded to a craft conception of the production process. This is apparent from the content of the 1972 training recommendations formulated by the SITB composed of employer and union representatives. The SITB's recommendations called for an initial year of 'common basic' training in which all craft-workers were given a basic appreciation of all phases of ship construction, both the hull-construction and outfitting stages (SITB 1972).

For the hull-construction trades, this initial year was to be followed by a further year in which a worker became versatile in all aspects of hull construction: welding, burning, caulking, assembling, drilling, and loftwork. Only at this stage, after two years of general training, would a metal-using worker specialize in one of three basic trade groups: caulker–burner–driller–riveter combined; plater–shipwright combined; or welder (SITB 1972: 13–16).[25]

The SITB's craft conception of the shipbuilding production process is unmistakable in its 1972 recommendations for the metal-using trades (SITB 1972: 7, 12):

The recommendations reflect the need for the craftsmen of the future to be versatile and adaptable and for training to facilitate the effective

---

[25] These training times can be usefully compared with those for welders and hull assemblers of the lowest grade at the Chantiers de la France in Dunkirk during the 1970s. Welders were recruited generally without prior experience and put on simple downhand production welding after a 16-week training period. Hull assemblers received an 8-week training course prior to being put on simple jobs. In both cases, on-the-job training was the primary means of skill acquisition. BETURE (1978: 84–6).

deployment of labour. This is obtained partly by broadly-based initial training, with appropriate specialization subsequently, and partly by 'supplementary' training on-the-job to assist flexibility and interchangeability.

The revised aim of common basic training is to give craft trainees a sufficient appreciation of the work of other crafts to enable them to co-ordinate their production work with that of other craftsmen in the interests of the job as a whole.

The limited impact of demarcation relaxation on industry-competitive performance raises the question of why organizational reform in the shipbuilding industry from the mid-1960s only amounted to a local modification of existing routines. In particular, it is striking that employers never acted to solve the increasingly severe problem of skilled labour shortage by upgrading less skilled workers. They continued to rely on skilled apprenticed workers for the co-ordination of the day-to-day process of production at the yard level.

Market constraints cannot provide the explanation. The state, in collaboration with the producers, reformed the industry's structure after 1965, and by the early 1970s most British yards were as specialized as their competitors abroad (see Ch. 4). In the concluding chapter I offer a reason for the localized nature of the modifications and consider its implications for general explanations for Britain's competitive decline.

6

Towards a Theory of British Economic Decline

THE explanation for the decline of British shipbuilding presented in Chapter 5 contained three parts: management's uncertainty over the need for organizational change; the political obstacles management faced to instituting change even when confronting a level of economic adversity that persuaded them of its necessity; the fact that when management achieved the necessary consensus to bring about change amongst the actors making up the firm, it proved to be too late. Reform arrived too late because, given the legacy of distrust between labour and management, the precondition for the changes to be seen as legitimate by all was the very process of ongoing bankruptcy and closure.

This concept of organizational rigidity can be put on a more sure theoretical footing by expanding the notion of enterprise organization as compromise and by integrating it into an evolutionary model of firm and industry response. My argument rests on the behavioural assumptions and conditions laid out in Chapter 1: bounded rationality, uncertainty, and the scope for opportunism in the context of strategic decision-making.

Two key background conditions of the analysis are specific to the case of British shipbuilding. The first concerns the fact that simply providing persuasive reasons why established firms might find it difficult or impossible to change does not explain the decline of a national industry faced by increasingly effective foreign competition. There must be a reason for the uniformity of the unchanging administrative practices among the firms making up the industry, including potential entrants. In the case of British shipbuilding, the strength of the collective organizations of both employers and workers at the national level and the interest of both groups in sustaining national-level collective-bargaining institutions provides such a reason.[1] In particular, new entrants were constrained to negotiate with the unions and to draw on a nationally organized work-force committed to maintaining established trade demarcations and working practices through collective action at the yard level.

Secondly, since greater ease of organizational change among competitors abroad is not assumed, different national industries must start in different places and be more or less well adapted to the changes which are occurring in the economic environment. Ample documentation has been presented in the earlier chapters to support this proposition in the case of the shipbuilding industry. British shipbuilders were distinguished internationally by their use of the craft system of work administration after World War II, a period when market and technical conditions favoured their competitors' bureaucratic systems.

I. A Constrained Evolutionary Model of Competitive Decline

To begin to understand the organization of the firm as truce or compromise is to appreciate the fact that most decisions of complex organizations require the co-operation of many individuals to be effective. Were interests identical and information about interests complete, the problematic aspect of carrying out decisions would be lack of trust in the competency of the actors, rather than lack of trust in their commitment to refrain from opportunistic behaviour.

One strand in the literature assumes a fundamental opposition of interests between labour and management and then resolves the problem of co-operation by assuming that all power resides

---

[1] The logic in this, from labour's perspective, is that organizing the entire relevant product market precludes firms outside the union's jurisdiction from offering competition that undermines collectively negotiated standards. In the case of a fragmented industry, such as British shipbuilding, the national level of trade-union organization will encourage similar national co-ordination among employers to preclude giving labour a 'whip-sawing' advantage in bargaining. A vast literature is available on the relation between bargaining power and bargaining structure. See e.g. Craypo (1986); Ulman (1974); Weber (1961).

with management (Braverman 1974; Gordon *et al.* 1982; Stone 1975). Management, they argue, devises internal control systems to monitor the behaviour of workers and to ensure that their behaviour conforms with the comprehensive instructions issued. Accepting, for the moment, this assumption about the way labour and management perceive their interests, the argument none the less falls down for a number of reasons. Even in the case of routinized work, bounded-rationality considerations preclude anticipating all contingencies in a work plan and correspondingly workers have to adapt their behaviour in ways that cannot be precisely specified in detailed instructions. Further, even on highly mechanized jobs, the efficiency of production rests in part on the workers' tacit knowledge about the idiosyncracies of particular machine processes. The effectiveness of work-to-rule strikes illustrates the importance of these potential sources of bargaining power (Crozier 1964: 187–98; Cyert and March 1963: 117–18; Matthewson 1969; Nelson and Winter 1982: 109–10). Also, there is no guarantee that supervisors will see their interests as identical to those of their employers. This poses an additional problem: Who will monitor the monitors?

For these reasons, regardless of whether the work-force is organized in trade unions or not, it can be argued that workers inevitably retain discretion over how they perform their jobs. Given this, and the radical assumption that the interests of management and labour are fundamentally opposed, the resulting vision of the firm is one of mutual defection in an iterated Prisoners' Dilemma.

While it is plausible to argue that workers and managers will see their interests as partly conflicting because of the zero sum property of the distribution of income at any point in time, it can also be argued that they will see a reason for co-operating to increase the total income available for future distribution. This nuanced conception of conflicting and mutual interests, combined with the idea that the conformity of workers' behaviour with the requirements of the organization depends on the employer having gained their consent, leads to an understanding of the firm as compromise or truce. The basis for compromise is that, though each side has an interest in altering the terms of their agreement to its advantage, both prefer maintaining the relation to breaking it off.

Thinking of organization as truce helps explain why adaptations to changing conditions may not easily be made and why organizations often retain the structures they had from their beginning. How do the individuals making up the organization understand proposals for adaptations? Are they efforts by one side to shift the terms of the agreement to their advantage? Or are they proposals for legitimate and mutually advantageous change? Given the less than complete information that usually characterizes such bargaining situations, and given the possibility of opportunistic behaviour, it is not surprising that proposed changes, even apparently quite easy ones, often meet with strong resistance and arouse suspicion. The result is that, in the absence of trust, existing routines and rules often become rigid, simply because no one wants to risk the consequences of breaking the truce.

In general, without trust, the nature and amount of resistance that can be anticipated to proposed administrative changes will depend on the type of change under consideration and on how well organized the work-force is. Changes which upset informally established relations of power among workers or between workers and supervisors are likely to provoke passive resistance at most, since, as a rule, the informality of such power structures gives them a doubtful legitimacy.[2] However, changes which subordinate workers to new authorities, such as introducing systematic management techniques, or changes which alter property rights to jobs, such as relaxing the lines of demarcation between occupational groups, are likely to provoke the opposition of trade unions. If the work-force is not organized in unions, such changes are likely to engender informal equivalents to formal union opposition, such as spontaneous walk-outs or work-to-rule strikes.[3]

In Chapter 1 I argued that organizations such as trade unions may serve efficiency purposes in situations in which the price system fails. The above discussion points to the naïvety of arguing that institutions will automatically serve these efficiency purposes. The problems of trust and opportunism at the heart of market failure may reappear inside the organization making it

---

[2] See, however, Terry (1977).
[3] These observations are based on Stinchcombe (1986: ch. 11).

difficult or impossible for firms to change their routine behaviour when faced with economic adversity. By integrating this idea of rigidity based on political constraints into an evolutionary model of firm and industry response, an explanation for economic decline emerges.

The standard formulation applying the evolutionary natural-selection approach to the capitalist firm is attributed to Alchian (1950). A key feature of the standard formulation in relation to neoclassical modelling of firm behaviour is the substitution of *ex post* selection and local optimization for *ex ante* maximizing rationality and global optimization. Firms are assumed to be operating in perfectly competitive markets and to be governed by rigid routines that are subject to random modifications rather than by rational decision-making. Assuming that the modifications are not too large and that selection operates at a sufficiently fast pace relative to the rate at which the environment is changing, it can be shown that the industry will move to a state in which all the surviving members of the group of firms use locally optimum techniques.[4]

Such an evolutionary model implies a radical rejection of the notion of rationality. In it there is no need to assume that decision-making is intentional, which is integral to the idea of bounded rationality used here. Bounded rationality implies that the actors aim to do as well as they can, taking into account their recognized limitations. The idea that decision-making is intentional, but prone to mistake, is in keeping with the spirit of the evolutionary approach. It is only essential to the evolutionary approach that the equilibrium results from the *ex post* selection of the consequences of behaviour rather than *ex ante* rational decision-making.[5]

---

[4] While in Alchian's formulation the equilibrium is an optimum, this is by no means necessary to the spirit of the approach. This might be the case for the simple, though rather uninteresting, reason that there are a number of equally and maximally good alternatives. See Elster (1983: 12) and Van Parijs (1981: 49–51).

[5] There must be some 'blindness' resulting in 'errors' in relation to the environment and criterion of selection, or else there will be nothing for selection to operate on. If errors are not possible, then it will be as if the equilibrium resulted from an omniscient actor weighing the expected consequences of a set of alternatives and choosing from among them according to a preference ordering.

The concept of bounded rationality in decision-making can be captured by introducing Herbert Simon's theory of 'satisficing' (1957), and the assumption that firms 'search', which has been developed in the work of Richard Nelson and Sidney Winter (1982). The assumption that firms 'satisfice', as opposed to optimize, is justified by Simon on the grounds of imperfect foresight and bounded-rationality considerations that preclude optimizing over the set of all conceivable alternatives.[6] Given these limits to rationality, all the firm can aim for is to do 'well enough'.

Search can be brought into a simple evolutionary model by assuming that the firm aims for a specified rate of return. As long as this rate is achieved, there is no change in routine behaviour. When gross returns fall below the satisficing level, however, the firm initiates a process of search, which is assumed to be local and is treated as stochastic.[7] Search may involve the introduction of new routines or the attempt to imitate the routines of more successful competitors. Though the contraction of less successful firms and the expansion of more successful firms, successful routines are progressively spread throughout the industry.

While it is possible to develop an equilibrium story in this manner, one of the advantages of the evolutionary approach, as Nelson and Winter point out, is the scope it offers for investigating firm behaviour under conditions of disequilibrium:

This kind of model can have an equilibrium with neoclassical properties, but it is also possible to explore the disequilibrium properties of the model, and indeed to set context such that equilibrium does not obtain over the entire relevant time span. While firms find better techniques, there always may be still better ones to be found. Profitable firms

---

[6] Sidney Winter (1964: 262) has developed a general argument demonstrating the impossibility of profit maximization. He argues that although there is an optimal amount of costly information that the firm should acquire to maximize profits, it is impossible for the firm to determine the amount. The choice of an information framework to make this decision itself requires information and, 'it is not apparent how the aspiring profit maximizer acquires this information or what guarantees that he does not pay an excessive price for it'. The infinite regress is cut short by assuming that the firm's goal is a 'satisfactory', as opposed to maximum, level of gross returns.

[7] In the simpler models of Nelson and Winter, it is assumed that the firm tests a random distribution of techniques in the neighbourhood of its current technique. See Nelson and Winter (1982: ch. 7) and Nelson *et al.* (1976).

expand, unprofitable ones contract. But the system need not drive out all but most efficient techniques and decision rules. Changes in the 'best' techniques known by firms and in the external environment of product demand and factor supply conditions may be sufficiently rapid relative to the speed of adjustment of the overall system that a wide range of behavior can survive at any time (Nelson and Winter 1975: 469).

Nelson and Winter assume that market selection operates upon routines and not the firm *per se*. Successful routines are spread throughout the economy not because less efficient firms close or go bankrupt, but because more efficient firms expand and the less efficient either successfully imitate them or contract in size. Disequilibrium obtains when the rate of change of the environment is more rapid that the rate at which less successful firms either imitate the more successful ones or contract in size.

If the speed at which firms adjust is rapid relative to the rate of change in the environment a satisficing equilibrium obtains. This differs from a neoclassical equilibrium in that firms of varying efficiencies may be operating. There is no motivation for a less efficient firm to change their routine behaviour in imitation or more profitable ones as long as their gross returns are greater than the satisficing level. The assumption that firms satisfice, rather than optimize, introduces an element of 'species inertia' into the analysis of firm and industry response.

Once the satisficing threshold has been crossed, however, the firm is very adaptable, only being constrained by bounded-rationality considerations (Mirowski 1983). For this reason the model cannot plausibly account for the long-term decline of a national industry relative to foreign competitors. To illustrate, let us pose the question: If British firms faced competition from foreign producers using superior routines, what would be the British industry's response once the rate of return fell below the satisficing level? Luck and varying entrepreneurial ability among firms introduce a stochastic element into the search process and correspondingly we would anticipate a distribution of firms in terms of their success in meeting the new competition. Some firms might collapse, but it is equally as probable that the search process would bring to light competitively superior routines. These would be no basis for expecting the British industry as a whole to decline relative to its competitors.

The problem with the evolutionary approach of Nelson and Winter for the purpose of explaining economic decline is that it doesn't incorporate enough species inertia. A theoretically consistent evolutionary explanation for decline must provide reasons why firms only adapt, if at all, when it is too late. The idea of institutional rigidity based on the fragility of the prevailing truce between labour and management provides such a reason. It can account for the failure of firms to initiate search even when gross returns fall below the satisficing level and gives the metaphor of natural selection applied to the problem of economic decline real bite.

The power of this constrained evolutionary conception of economic development and stagnation can be appreciated by considering its relevance to the case of shipbuilding. While imperfect foresight meant that British builders during the decade or so following World War II were uncertain that changing market conditions would undermine the profitability of their established routines, they were certain that if they attempted to alter the rules defining the truce they would run into trouble with a well-organized work-force that would view any proposed reform as a trap. Under these conditions, it was reasonable for British producers not to change. They only acted to change their established routines when economic difficulties were sufficiently close. This was not to push laggard men into action, but to persuade all the actors that the failure to undertake organizational reform would result in the collapse of the industry. At that time British builders succeeded in building up trust with their work-force around proposed institutional reforms.

This interpretation of the failure to change, which places considerable emphasis on political constraints, is supported by the fact that there was a significant fall in industrial profit margins from the late 1950s, but change only came about during the second half of the 1960s, following the closure in 1963 of such major producers as Denny and Bros., W. Hamilton, and the Harland and Wolff's Govan yard, and the financial collapse in 1965 of the Fairfields yard.[8] It was only after 1965 that the unions

[8] According to a private survey conducted by Hoare and Co., the industry profit/sales ratio fell from 6.4% in 1958 to 2.4% in 1964. See Slaven (1981*a*: 21).

at the national level accepted the need for organizational reform and actively promoted productivity bargaining at the local level.

There is also strong evidence that political constraints played a role in determining the content of the organizational reforms. For example, by the early 1960s British builders were well aware that their increasingly successful competitors were using fundamentally different management techniques. The 1962 industry-commissioned Patton Report pinpointed the underdeveloped nature of managerial hierarchies in the industry as a serious weakness and recommended a more systematic approach to production control.[9] Despite this, the 1973 Booz-Allen and Hamilton Report, commissioned by the Department of Trade and Industry, showed that no significant changes in the degree of managerial control over shop-floor production had taken place during the preceding decade.

British producers' inexperience with systematic management techniques no doubt would have meant that any attempt to imitate the routines of more successful Scandinavian or French builders would have resulted in an organizational variation with distinct national characteristics. The fact that the post-1965 organizational reforms only amounted to local modifications of the craft system, however, can best be accounted for by the need to find a set of changes that both labour and management perceived as mutually beneficial. In this regard, it is not surprising that management never acted to resolve the increasingly severe skilled labour shortages of the 1960s by upgrading less skilled workers. These measures would have been unacceptable to the craft-unions since they would have displaced their members from the production process. The local nature of the modifications should not be understood as resulting primarily from a lack of information about alternatives, but rather from the politics of negotiating mutually acceptable change.

The emphasis I have placed on political constraints and compromise among the actors is a significant departure from the main thrust of most evolutionary modelling. The resulting vision of the shipbuilding industry's development and the competitive decline

---

[9] Also see the *Shipbuilder and Marine Engine Builder* (Apr. 1962: 210; Jan. 1964: 10).

of the British, however, is not out of keeping with the spirit of the evolutionary approach. Happenstance and uncertainty did play a role in the shifting fortunes of shipbuilders after World War II. But the failure of the British to change should not be understood solely in terms of British management's blindness, much less their incompetency. British businessmen may have been lucky when they succeeded, but they were not stupid when they failed, just constrained by lack of trust.

II. Implications for Historical Research

In considering the implications of this argument for historical research on British economic decline, it is fortunate that some of the necessary groundwork has been done. The volume edited by Bernard Elbaum and William Lazonick (1986) provides persuasive testimony for a number of key British industries (steel, motor vehicles, and cotton textiles) that competitive decline can be attributed, at least in part, to the failure to transform institutional arrangements at the enterprise level, and in particular the failure to adopt bureaucratic methods of work administration suitable for mass production (Elbaum and Lazonick 1986: 8, 24–7, 69–71, 149–53).[10]

If this argument is accepted, then one of the most important implications of this study is the need to examine individual industries for the relation between the behaviour of British entrepreneurs and their beliefs under conditions of uncertainty. This research agenda can be divided into two parts: (1) the beliefs of management about uncertain market states and how they affected their perception of the need for institutional reform; (2) the beliefs of management and labour about each other in strategic settings, and whether distrust effectively blocked co-operation around proposed reforms.

With respect to the first part, ideally we would want to identify key turning-points in market conditions for each industry, such as the 1950s in shipbuilding. During this period the international

---

[10] Also see Elbaum and Wilkinson (1979); Lazonick (1979); Lewchuck (1987: chs. 8, 9); Lewchuck (1989); Williams *et al.* (1983); Wilkinson (1989).

competitive environment was transformed through the successful pursuit by Swedish and Japanese shipbuilders of mass-production strategies based on bureaucratic methods of work administration. The increasing acceptance of standardized vessels in internationally competitive markets progressively undermined the competitive position of the British shipbuilders who relied on the craft system of work administration that was more suitable for producing customized products.

In this regard, the key question would be: Can the initial failure of British management to change be explained by the quite reasonable decision to follow established rules of thumb under conditions of market uncertainty?[11] A related question is: Was management's uncertainty over the need for change heightened by various market imperfections which conferred, at least temporarily, a protected position in the domestic market?

With regard to the second part of the agenda, did the level of economic adversity (loss of domestic-market share and declining profitability) at some point become sufficient to persuade management of the need for institutional reform? To ask this in the language of evolutionary economics: did the time come when gross returns fell below the satisficing level? A subsequent failure to change raises the issue of the beliefs of the actors about each other and a possible failure of mutually beneficial co-operation.

At this point in our argument, there are two key questions to pose: Did mutually agreed reform stumble against the obstacle of labour's distrust of the motivation behind management's proposed reforms? Given the legacy of distrust, what was needed to persuade labour to change their beliefs concerning management's trustworthiness? If, as occurred in the shipbuilding industry, the required evidence was something perceived by labour as external to the firm (bankruptcy or closure), then tragically, inevitably, the tendency would be for reform to be enacted too late.

A related question is whether the greater success of producers abroad can be interpreted as a fortuitous fitting of already existing institutional arrangements into an altered competitive

---

[11] See Heiner (1983: 568–70) and Hey (1981: 62–3) who, in the spirit of Simon's theory of satisficing, argue for the reasonableness of following rules of thumb under conditions of uncertainty.

environment. This appears to have been the case for Scandinavian and Continental shipbuilders after World War II.

Alternatively, it is possible that some nations embody a higher level of trust in their industrial-relations systems than others, facilitating the process of ongoing adaptation to a changing environment. There is some evidence to suggest this is the case for Japan (Dore 1986 and 1987).

As Fox (1985: p. xi) has pointed out, distrust is not absolute in the British system of industrial relations. Relations between labour and management have shown a continual win–lose posture, which none the less rarely has manifested itself in destructively aggressive stances by employers or revolutionary positions by workers. There is enough trust to produce the necessary co-operation to sustain production, but not enough for workers to forgo the creation of narrow substantive rules, which managerial slackness allows, designed to protect them from an abuse of authority. In the Japanese system, by contrast, workers' expectation of the possibility of power being exercised with benevolence encourages them to forgo the creation of narrow substantive rules which impede adaptability:

Two things follow from the dominance of such an ideology in a society [Japan] . . . First, . . . some people *must* be induced by internalized norms of conscience to be more responsible in the exercise of power than they otherwise would be. Secondly, given the expectation on the part of subordinates of the *possibility* of power being exercised with benevolence, benevolence actually becomes an efficient strategy for the retention of power. In such a society, a little benevolence can go a long way to evoking trust, much farther than in a society where expectations are lower and suspicion of power more deeply ingrained (Dore 1987: 94–5).

This suggests an evolutionary model different from that presented above, where the flexible producers, though less well suited to the model environment than the more rigid ones, have greater survival capacity in a fluctuating environment (Nelson and Winter 1982: 161).

Finally, there are some interesting parallels and important differences between the explanation for decline developed here and the competing explanations outlined in Chapter 1. In common with the entrepreneurial-failure thesis, I argue that the process of belief formation is key. The entrepreneurial-failure thesis argues that a cultural mechanism operating 'behind our backs' resulted in biased-belief formation and incorrect estimates of the costs and benefits associated with various opportunities. By contrast, in the argument elaborated here, the beliefs of the actors are seen as substantially rational in the sense of being grounded in available evidence (see Elster 1983: 1–5).

For example, the tendency of British shipbuilders to discount the suitability of bureaucratic methods of work administration during the early 1950s was reasonable under conditions of uncertainty. When industrial profit margins declined during the late 1950s, they altered their beliefs about the need for administrative change (see Chapter 5).

Similarly, the initial failure of labour to co-operate with management's proposed reforms should not be attributed to an irrational 'bloody-mindedness'. Recent work in game-theory on the iterated Prisoners' Dilemma has shown that even in a situation where both actors are conditional co-operators, the failure of co-operation to emerge is consistent with rational behaviour. If one side believes the other side to be an unconditional defector, or believes that the other side believes that he is an unconditional defector, then mutual defection can be the result even when all would prefer co-operation (Axelrod 1984; Binmore and Dasgupta 1986: 233–4).

Given the legacy of adversarial industrial relations in the British shipbuilding industry, it was reasonable that workers should be cautious of management's proposed reforms demanding short-term sacrifices for future joint benefits. The substantial evidence provided by firm bankruptcies and closures during the early 1960s led labour to alter their beliefs concerning the trustworthiness of managerial initiatives (see Chapter 5).

In comparison with the rational-choice explanation for decline based on the assumption of optimizing rationality, there is an evident loss of parsimony in the explanation proposed here. Further, as the critics have noted, the notions of satisficing and search are more *ad hoc* descriptions than theoretical constructs (Elster 1989: 26–35). In this light, one of the contributions of this study is to provide an explanation for the localized nature of search which is not *ad hoc*. It can be explained by the political constraint of finding a set of changes that are acceptable to both labour and management in a bilateral monopoly situation.

A related point is that under conditions of uncertainty, the determinacy of optimizing models can only be retained through making equally *ad hoc* assumptions. For example, the notion of 'satisficing' provides a partial solution to the problem of choice given bounded rationality considerations. However, satisficing can be reinterpreted as a problem of maximizing subject to assumed constraints on available information. Alternatively, the problem of uncertainty over states of the world can be resolved by assuming the actors have particular subjective probability distributions (Myerson 1985).

Ultimately, there is a trade-off. My explanation for decline embodies greater behavioural realism than the rational-choice one, but at the expense of some loss of parsimony. Whether the greater insight into the actual mechanisms of decline justifies the loss is a question I leave for the reader.

APPENDIX A

Statistical Tables

TABLE A.1. Launching of ships over 100 gross registered tons in Britain and France

Year[a]	Britain		France	
	Output 000s tons	%age of world output	Output 000s tons	%age of world output
1892	1,110	81.7	17	1.3
1893	836	81.4	20	1.9
1894	1,047	79.0	20	1.5
1895	951	78.0	28	2.3
1896	1,160	74.0	45	2.9
1897	925	69.4	49	3.7
1898	1,368	72.3	67	3.5
1899	1,417	66.7	90	4.2
1900	1,442	62.5	117	5.1
1901	1,525	58.2	178	6.8
1902	1,428	57.0	192	7.7
1903	1,191	55.5	93	4.3
1904	1,205	59.5	81	4.0
1905	1,623	64.5	73	2.9
1906	1,828	62.6	35	1.2
1907	1,607	58.0	62	2.0
1908	930	50.7	83	4.7
1909	991	62.0	42	2.6
1910	1,143	58.4	81	4.0
1911	1,804	68.0	125	4.7
1912	1,738	60.0	111	3.8
1913	1,932	58.0	176	5.3
1914	1,648	59.0	114	5.2
1919	1,620	22.6	33	0.4
1920	2,056	35.0	93	1.5
1921	1,538	41.8	211	4.8
1922	1,031	41.2	185	7.4

TABLE A.1. (cont'd)

Year[a]	Britain		France	
	Output 000s tons	%age of world output	Output 000s tons	%age of world output
1923	646	39.2	97	5.9
1924	1,440	64.1	80	3.5
1925	1,085	49.5	76	3.4
1926	640	38.2	121	7.2
1927	1,226	53.0	44	1.9
1928	1,446	53.6	81	3.0
1929	1,523	54.5	82	2.9
1930	1,479	51.2	101	3.4
1931	502	31.1	103	6.3
1932	188	25.8	89	12.3
1933	133	27.2	34	6.9
1934	460	47.5	16	1.5
1935	499	38.3	43	3.2
1936	856	40.4	39	1.8
1937	921	34.2	27	0.9
1938	1,030	34.0	47	1.5
1948	1,176	51.1	138	6.0
1949	1,267	40.5	155	5.0
1950	1,325	37.9	181	5.2
1951	1,341	36.8	223	6.1
1952	1,303	29.6	213	4.4
1953	1,317	25.8	235	4.6
1954	1,409	26.8	267	5.1
1955	1,474	27.7	326	6.1
1956	1,383	20.7	298	4.5
1957	1,414	16.6	429	5.0
1958	1,402	15.1	451	4.9
1959	1,373	15.7	408	4.7
1960	1,331	16.0	446	5.3
1961	1,192	15.0	480	6.0
1962	1,073	12.8	447	5.3
1963	928	10.9	510	6.1
1964	1,043	10.2	479	4.7
1965	1,073	8.8	443	3.6
1966	1,084	7.6	553	3.9

TABLE A.1. (cont'd)

Year[a]	Britain		France	
	Output 000s tons	%age of world output	Output 000s tons	%age of world output
1967	1,298	8.2	490	3.1
1968	898	5.3	791	4.7
1969	1,040	5.4	960	5.0
1970	1,237	5.7	1,112	5.1

[a] Please note that returns were not published during the First and Second World Wars.

Source: Lloyd's Register of Shipping, Annual Shipbuilding Returns.

TABLE A.2. Vessels launched from Loire-Inférieure, 1900–1936

Year	Loire-Inférieure	
	Number	%age of French output
1900	82,136	70.1
1901	114,454	64.3
1902	99,042	51.6
1903	38,823	41.7
1904	41,781	51.6
1905	n/a	n/a
1906	25,461	34.9
1907	n/a	n/a
1908	26,459	31.9
1909	n/a	n/a
1910	3,316	4.1
1911	21,792	17.4
1912	62,510	56.3
1913	83,363	47.4
1914	14,364	12.6
1915	14,371	n/a
1916	n/a	n/a
1917	n/a	n/a
1918	n/a	n/a
1919	8,085	24.5

TABLE A.2. (cont'd)

Year	Loire-Inférieure	
	Number	%age of French output
1920	27,324	29.4
1921	40,344	19.0
1922	36,692	19.8
1923	21,672	22.3
1924	20,832	26.0
1925	36,792	48.4
1926	68,458	56.6
1927	17,634	40.0
1928	10,283	12.7
1929	28,221	34.4
1930	n/a	n/a
1931	33,501	32.5
1932	68,408	76.9
1933	8,399	24.7
1934	3,832	23.8
1935	19,262	44.9
1936	34,484	88.5

Sources: Lloyd's Register of Shipping, Annual Shipbuilding Returns; Thebault (1979: 71).

TABLE A.3. Output of tankers in Britain and the world, 1921–1970. (000s tons launched)

Year	Britain			World	
	Tonnage launched	As %age of all tonnage launched	As %age world tanker output	Tonnage launched	As %age of all tonnage launched
1921	251	16.3	23.9	1,050	24.1
1922	263	25.5	73.9	356	14.4
1923	58	9.0	46.0	126	7.6
1924	65	45.1	56.0	116	5.2
1925	135	12.4	47.0	287	13.1
1926	100	16.0	40.6	246	14.7
1927	305	24.9	56.3	542	23.7

TABLE A.3. (cont'd)

Year	Britain			World	
	Tonnage launched	As %age of all tonnage launched	As %age world tanker output	Tonnage launched	As %age of all tonnage launched
1928	300	20.7	46.4	647	24.0
1929	175	11.4	54.0	324	11.6
1930	550	37.2	61.8	890	30.8
1931	242	48.2	37.6	643	39.8
1932	6	3.2	4.4	135	18.6
1933	—	0.0	0.0	83	17.0
1934	69	15.0	34.8	198	20.5
1935	51	10.2	15.1	338	26.0
1936	149	17.4	22.3	668	31.6
1937	145	15.7	118.8	770	28.9
1948	291	24.7	48.6	600	26.0
1949	434	34.3	32.5	1,336	42.7
1950	614	46.4	38.9	1,579	41.6
1951	834	62.2	54.2	1,538	42.2
1952	643	49.4	32.1	2,002	45.6
1953	762	57.9	26.6	2,862	56.9
1954	714	50.7	24.6	2,899	55.2
1955	648	44.0	26.5	2,437	45.9
1956	516	37.5	22.8	2,267	34.0
1957	535	37.9	13.9	3,851	45.3
1958	577	41.2	15.0	4,775	51.4
1959	529	38.6	12.1	4,375	50.0
1960	618	46.4	16.9	3,649	43.7
1961	393	35.7	14.0	2,803	35.5
1962	403	37.6	14.3	2,998	35.8
1963	369	39.8	9.9	3,716	43.5
1964	420	40.3	7.6	5,529	53.9
1965	421	39.2	7.8	5,393	44.2
1966	244	23.6	4.6	5,354	37.4
1967	265	20.4	5.2	5,114	32.4
1968	351	39.0	5.3	6,613	39.1
1969	513	49.3	5.5	9,325	48.3
1970	575	46.5	5.7	10,031	46.2

Source: Lloyd's Register of Shipping, Annual Shipbuilding Returns.

APPENDIX B

Glossary of Technical Terms

AMIDSHIP: Section of a ship half-way between bow and stern.

BATTEN: A thin strip of wood used in measuring or making templates.

BEAM: An athwartship member supporting a portion of a deck. Also the width of the ship.

BEAM-BRACKET: Plate at ends of beam, riveted to beam and frame.

BENDING FLOOR: Large iron floor on which frames are bent.

BENDING ROLLS: Large machine used to give curvature to plates.

BENDING SLAB: Heavy cast-iron blocks arranged to form a large solid floor on which angles are bent.

BEVEL: The angle between the flanges of a frame and other member. (When greater than a right angle, 'open bevel'; when less, 'closed'.)

BILGE: The rounded portion of the hull between the side and bottom.

BOTTOM: Portion of the hull below the bilge.

BRIDGE: The athwartship platform above the weather-deck from which the ship is steered, navigated, etc.

BRIDGE-DECK: Partial deck extending from side to side of ship, located about amidship.

BULKHEAD: A vertical partition corresponding to the wall of a building, extending either athwartships or fore-and-aft, and separating one compartment from the other.

CAULK: To make watertight or oil-tight.

COLLAR: A flanged band or ring.

COUNTERSINK: The taper of a rivet-hole for a flush rivet.

DEADWEIGHT: The total weight of cargo, fuel, water, stores, passengers and crew, and their effects, that a ship can carry.

DECK: The part of a ship that corresponds to the floor of a building.

DERRICK: A device for hoisting heavy weights, cargo, etc.

DISPLACEMENT: The total weight of the ship when afloat, including everything on board; the volume of water displaced by a ship.

DOUBLE BOTTOM: Compartments at bottom of ship between inner and outer bottoms, used for ballast tanks, water, fuel, oil, etc.

FAIR: Smooth without abruptness or unevenness, in agreement. Fairing the lines consists in making them smooth. Rivet-holes are fair when they agree one with another in adjoining members.

FLANGE: Portion of plate or shape at, or nearly at, right angles to main portion.

FORECASTLE: The forward, upper portion of the hull, generally used for the crew's quarters.

FORGING: A mass of steel worked to a special shape by hammering while red-hot.

FRAMES: Upright members or ribs forming the skeleton of a ship.

GROSS TONNAGE: A figure obtained by dividing the total volume of the ship, in cubic feet, by 100.

HULL: The body of a ship, including shell plating and frames.

JOGGLING: Offsetting the edges of plates of outer strakes to avoid the use of 'liners'.

KEEL: The fore-and-aft member, usually in the form of flat plates end to end, extending from stem or stern along the bottom of a ship on the centre line.

KEEL BLOCKS: Heavy blocks on which ship rests during construction.

LAP: A joint in which one part overlaps the other, thus avoiding the use of a butt strap.

LAYING OFF: Marking plates, shapes, etc., for shearing and punching from template.

LIFT: To lift a template is to make it from measurement given and also to suit conditions.

LINER: Generally a small tapered plate fitted between plates at a lap, sometimes of parallel thickness for outside plates.

LINES: The plans of a ship that show its form. From the lines, drawn full size on the mould-loft floor, are made templates of the various parts of the hull.

MOULD: A light pattern of a part of a ship. Usually made of thin wood or paper. Also called a template, for laying out plates or shapes.

MOULD-LOFT: A shed or building with large, smooth floor on which the lines of a ship can be drawn to full scale and templates lifted.

NET TONNAGE: A figure obtained by making deduction from the gross tonnage to allow for space not available for carrying cargo.

RIB-BAND: A fore-and-aft wooden strip or heavy batten used to support the transverse frames temporarily after erection.

RIVET: A short steel bolt usually driven or clinched after being heated red-hot.

RUDDER: A large fitting hinged to the rudder-post. Used for steering the ship.

RUDDER-POST: The vertical post at after-end of stern-frame which supports rudder.

SCANTLINGS: The dimensions of various parts of the ship.

SCRIVE-BOARD: A large section of flooring in the mould-loft in which the lines of the body-plan are cut in with a knife. Used for making moulds of the frames, beams, floor plates, etc.

SET IRON: Bar of soft iron used on bending slab to give shape of frames.

STERN-FRAME: Large casting attached to after-end of keel to form ship's stern. Often includes rudder-post, stern-post, and aperture for propeller.

STRAKE: A fore-and-aft course or row of shell or deck plating.

TEMPLATE: Full-sized pattern.

VLCC: Very large crude carrier. Generally defined as a tanker over 100,000 deadweight tons.

Bibliography

Archive Sources

British

SRNA Archives, National Maritime Museum, Greenwich:
London Minute Books.
Federation Circulars.
Part 1, No. 10, file 4092, 'Returns of Numbers of Employees in the Shipbuilding and Repairing Industry'.
Part II, No. 17, file 3198, 'Demarcation Questions'.
Part II, No. 17, file 5007, 'Machine Manning'.
'Statistics of the Shipbuilding, Shiprepairing and Marine Engineering Industries, 1920–1939', prepared by the Shipbuilding Conference.
The SRNA was formed in 1967 through the merger of the Shipbuilding Conference (founded in 1928), the SEF (founded in 1899), and the Dry Dock Owners' and Repairers' Central Council (founded in 1910). The archives contain the extant collection of records of these organizations. For a description of their holdings and a guide to the records of British shipbuilding companies, the reader should refer to L. A. Ritchie, *Modern British Shipbuilding: A Guide to Historical Records* (Maritime Monograph No. 48; National Maritime Museum, 1980).

Bank of England Central Archive, Accession no. 1/1020: 'Memo of Meeting of Mortagu Norman with Shipbuilding Conference Deputation', Mar. 1929.
University of Glasgow Archives, UCS 3, 'The Records of Alexander Stephen and Sons, Glasgow':
UCS 3/1/186, 'Report on Shipwright/Boilermaker Demarcation Dispute', June–Sept. 1957.
Modern Records Centre, University of Warwick, Confederation of Shipbuilding and Engineering Unions Records: MSS 44/TBN 15, File 3, 'Financial Report on Shipbuilding and Allied Companies', prepared by *The Economist*, 10 Feb. 1954.
TUC Library, Shipbuilding File (1933). 'Shipbuilding Employers Association Proceedings in General Conference with the Federation of Engineering and Shipbuilding Trades', 1 Nov.

French

Archives nationales, Paris, Series F7, 'Police générale':
F7 13606 'États de syndicats'.
Archives départmental de la Loire-Atlantique, Nantes: Series 1 M 2339,
'Bordereaux de salaires, chômage, accords et salaires'.
Archives des ateliers et chantiers de Provence, Centre culturel, Port-de-
Bouc (1953). Corporate and labour records: 'Rapport d'une mission à
Kochums'.

Official Publications

British

Royal Commission on Depression in Trade (1886). (C. 4621), xxi–xxiii.
Booth Committee (1918). Board of Trade, Departmental Committee on
Shipping and Shipbuilding after the War (Cd. 9092).
Ministry of Labour (1927–8). *Report of an Enquiry into Apprenticeship
and Training for Skilled Occupations in Great Britain and Northern
Ireland, 1925–1926* (HMSO).
Board of Trade (1932). *Industrial Survey, Southwest of Scotland.*
Department of Scientific and Industrial Research (1960). 'Research and
Development Requirements of the Shipbuilding and Marine Engineer-
ing Industries'.
Gedden Report (1965–6). *Report of the Shipbuilding Inquiry Committee*
(Cmnd. 2937), vii.
SITB (1966–7). 'Report and Statement of Accounts', xxxviii.
SITB (1967–8). 'Report and Statement of Accounts', xxiv.
Donovan Commission (1965–8). *Report of the Royal Commission on
Trade Unions and Employers' Associations* (Cmnd. 3623).
Commission on Industrial Relations (1970–1). *Report no. 22: Shipbuild-
ing and Shiprepairing* (Cmnd. 4756), xxv.
SITB (1972). 'Recommendations for the Training of Shipyard Metal-
Using Trainees' (Training Policy Statement No. 3; Aug.).
Booz-Allen and Hamilton Report (1973). 'British Shipbuilding 1972',
Report to the Department of Trade and Industry.
Northern Region Strategy Team Working Paper (1976). 'Settlement
Patterns and Policies in the Tyne and Wear', Project No. B1A
Newcastle-upon-Tyne, Mar.

French

Enquête du Conseil national économique (1930). *Situation de l'industrie
de la construction navale, 1929–1930* (Chambre syndicale des construc-
tures de navires, circulaire 11B; Paris).

Commissariat générale du plan (1976). 'La Construction navale', vii^è plan (La Documentation française, Paris).
BETURE (1978). 'Les Ouvriers de la siderurgie et de la métallurgie à Dunkerque', Secretariat d'état aux transports' (Trappes, June).

Other

League of Nations (1927). 'Memorandum of Shipbuilding' (Geneva).

Periodical Publications

British

Census of Population for England and Wales (1951).
Department of Employment Gazette (1966 and 1975).
Ministry of Labour and National Services Employment Exchange (1960). 'Returns of Shipbuilding and Ship-Repairing'.

French

INSEE (1963). Rencensement de l'industrie: résultats pour 1962.

Reports of Organizations

AREMORS (1983). *Études et documents sur Saint-Nazaire et le mouvement ouvrier de 1920–1939* (Imprimerie Atlantique, Saint-Nazaire).
H. P. Drewry Ltd. (Shipping Consultants, Landa), 'Shipbuilding Credits and Government Aid' (1972–3).
—— 'The Role of the EEC in World Shipbuilding' (1974).
Patton Report (1962). 'Productivity and Research in Shipbuilding', Report prepared under the Chairmanship of Mr J. Patton to the Joint Committee of the Shipbuilding Conference, the Shipbuilding Employers Association, and the British Shipbuilding Research Association.
SSA Executive Committee Reports (1933, 1934, 1944).

Books Articles and Theses

ABAUT, A. (1913). 'Travail d'usine', *Revue de métallurgie*, 10.
ABELL, W. A. (1948). *The Shipwright's Trade* (Cambridge University Press, Cambridge).

ALCHIAN, A. (1950). 'Uncertainty, Evolution and Economic Theory', *Journal of Political Economy*, 58.

ALDCROFT, D. H. (1964). 'The Entrepreneur and the British Economy, 1870–1914', *Economic History Review*^{2}, 17.

—— (1968). *The Development of British and Foreign Competition, 1875–1914* (George Allen and Unwin, London).

ALEXANDER, K. J. W. and JENKINS, C. L. (1970). *Fairfields: A Study of Industrial Change* (Allen Lane, London).

ALLEN, R. (1979). 'International Competition in Iron and Steel, 1850–1913', *Journal of Economic History*, 39.

ARROW, K. (1974). *The Limits of Organization* (W. W. Norton, New York).

—— (1984). *Individual Choice under Uncertainty* (Harvard University Press, Cambridge, Mass.).

AXELROD, R. (1984). *The Evolution of Cooperation* (Basic Books, New York).

BARBANCE, M. (1948). 'Saint Nazaire: le port la ville, le travail', Thèse pour le Doctorat en Droit (Faculté de Droit, Université de Rennes).

BASSO, L. (1910). 'Les Enterprises françaises de construction navales', Thèse pour le Doctorat en Droit (Faculté de Droit, Université de Paris).

BENOIST, C. (1905). *L'Organisation du travail: la crise de l'état moderne*, (Librarie Plon, Paris).

BERTIN, L. E. (1884). 'Rapport sur une seconde mission en Angleterre, 5 août–15 sept. 1884' (Collection de la Bibliothèque de la marine marchande, Paris).

BINMORE, K. and DASGUPTA, P. (1986). *Economic Organizations as Games* (Oxford University Press, Oxford).

BLOCH, M. (1952). *Les Caractères originaux de l'histoire rurale française* (Armand Colin, Paris).

—— (1967). *Seigneurie française et manoir anglais* (Armand Colin, Paris).

BOEKHOLT, R. (1971). 'Welding: A Key Factor in Shipbuilding', *Shipbuilding International* (Sept.).

BOYER, G. (1988). 'What Did Unions Do in Nineteenth Century Britain?', *Journal of Economic History*, 48.

BRAVERMAN, H. (1974). *Labour and Monopoly Capital* (Monthly Review Press, New York).

BRIEUX, M. (1972). 'Le Mouvement ouvrier à Nantes de 1919 à 1931', Mémoire de Maîtrise (Université de Nantes).

BROWN, A. J. (1972). *The Framework of Regional Economics in the United Kingdom* (Cambridge University Press, Cambridge).

BROWN, R., BRANNEN, P., COUSINS, J. M., and SAMPLER, M. L. (1972). 'The Contours of Solidarity: Social Stratification and Industrial Relations in Shipbuilding', *British Journal of Industrial Relations*, 10.

BURET, J. (1968). 'L'evolution de la specialisation des Chantiers navales de la Ciotat dans le domaine des navires transports de gaz', *Nouveautés techniques maritimes*.

BURN, D. (1940). *Economic History of Steel Making, 1867–1939* (Cambridge University Press, Cambridge).

CAIRNCROSS, A. K. and PARKINSON, J. R. (1958). 'The Shipbuilding Industry', in D. Burn (ed.), *The Structure of British Industry: A Symposium*, ii (Cambridge University Press, Cambridge).

CARON, F. (1974). *An Economic History of Modern France* (Columbia University Press, New York).

CARRÉ, J.-J., DUBOIS, P., and MALINVAUD, E. (1976). *French Economic Growth* (Oxford University Press, Oxford).

CHANDLER, A. (1977). *The Visible Hand* (Harvard University Press, Cambridge, Mass.).

CHARDONNET, J. (1971). *L'Économie française: les grandes industries*, ii (Dalloz, Paris).

CHARPENTIER, H. (1945). *La Construction de navires marchands* (Dunod, Paris).

CHARPY, G. (1919). 'Essai d'organisation méthodique dans une usine métallurgique', *Bulletin de la société d'encouragement pour l'industrie nationale*, 118: 1.

CHASSERIAU, R. (1901). *De la protection de l'industrie des construction navale*, Thèse pour le Doctorat en Droit (Faculté de Droit, Université de Paris).

CHILD, J. (1967). *Industrial Relations in the British Print Industry* (George Allen and Unwin, London).

CHUSSEAU, Y. (1977). 'Le Mouvement ouvrier à Nantes de 1936 à août 1939', Mémoire de Maîtrise (Université de Nantes).

CLAPHAM, J. H. (1968). *The Economic Development of France and Germany, 1815–1919* (4th edn., Cambridge University Press, Cambridge).

CLEGG, H. A. (1964). *General Union in a Changing Society* (Basil Blackwell, Oxford).

—— (1979). *The Changing System of Industrial Relations in Great Britain* (Basil Blackwell, Oxford).

—— FOX, A., and THOMPSON, E. F. (1964). *A History of British Trade Unions since 1889*, i. *1889–1910* (Clarendon Press, Oxford).

COATES, D. and HILLARD, J. (eds.), *The Economic Decline of Modern Britain* (Harvester Wheatsheaf, Hemel Hempstead).

COLEMAN, D. C. (1973). 'Gentlemen and Players', *Economic History Review*, NS 26.

COMPAGNON, J. (1919). 'L'Atelier central de réparation des automobiles', *Bulletin de la société d'encouragement pour l'industrie nationale*, 118: 1.

COPPOCK, D. J. (1956). 'The Climacteric of the 1890s: A Critical Note', *Manchester School*, 24.

CORMACK, W. S. (1930). 'An Economic History of Shipbuilding and Marine Engineering with Special Reference to the West of Scotland', Ph.D. thesis (University of Glasgow).

CRAFTS, N. F. R. (1984). 'Economic Growth in France and Britain, 1830–1910: A Review of the Evidence', *Journal of Economic History*, 44.

—— (1985). *British Economic Growth during the Industrial Revolution* (Oxford University Press, Oxford).

CRAIG, J. (1917–18). 'Some Effects of War on Merchant Shipbuilding', *Transactions of the Institution of Engineers and Shipbuilders in Scotland*, 61.

CRAYPO, C. (1986). *The Economics of Collective Bargaining* (BNA Book, Washington, DC).

CROZIER, M. (1964). *The Bureaucratic Phenomenon* (Chicago University Press, Chicago).

CUTHBERT, D. (1969). 'Welding in Modern Ship Construction', *Welding and Metal Fabrication* (exhibition number, Apr.).

CYERT, R. M. and MARCH, J. G. (1963). *A Behavioral Theory of the Firm* (Prentice Hall, Englewood Cliffs, NJ).

DENISON, E. F. (1967). *Why Growth Rates Differ* (The Brookings Institute, Washington, DC).

—— (1968). 'Economic Growth', in R. E. Caves and Associates, *Britain's Economic Prospects* (George Allen and Unwin, London).

DE RAM (1909). 'Note sur un essai d'application du système Taylor dans un grand atelier de mécanique (Usines Renault)', *Revue de métallurgie*, 6.

DEVINAT, P. (1927). 'Scientific Management in Europe' (ILO Studies and Reports, Series B, No. 17; Geneva).

DORE, R. (1986). *Flexible Rigidities: Industrial Policy Adjustment in Japan* (Athlone Press, London).

—— (1987). *Taking Japan Seriously* (Stanford University Press, Stanford).

DOUGAN, D. (1975). *The Shipwrights* (F. Graham, Newcastle-upon-Tyne).

DUBIGEON, G. (1928). 'Du salaire ouvrière dans la métallurgie nantaise de 1914 à 1927', Thèse pour le Doctorat en Droit (Faculté de Droit, Université de Rennes).

DUGAS, R. (1930). 'L'Industrie de la construction navale', Enquête du Conseil national économique, *Situation de l'industrie de la construction navale, 1929–1930.*

ELBAUM, B. (1986). 'The Steel Industry before World War I', in Elbaum and Lazonick (eds.), *The Decline of the British Economy.*

—— (1989). 'Why Apprenticeship Persisted in Britain but not in the United States', *Journal of Economic History*, 49.

—— and LAZONICK, W. (1986). *The Decline of the British Economy* (Oxford University Press, Oxford).

—— and WILKINSON, F. (1979). 'Industrial Relations and Uneven Development: A Comparison Study of the American and British Steel Industries', *Cambridge Journal of Economics*, 3.

ELDRIDGE, J. E. T. (1968). *Industrial Disputes* (Routledge and Kegan Paul, London).

ELSTER, J. (1979). *Ulysses and the Sirens: Studies in Rationality and Irrationality* (Cambridge University Press, Cambridge).

—— (1983). *Sour Grapes: Studies in the Subversion of Rationality* (Cambridge University Press, Cambridge).

—— (1989). *The Cement of Society* (Cambridge University Press, Cambridge).

FAIRBURN, W. A. (1902). 'Methods of Handling Material over Shipbuilding Berths in American Shipyards', *Transactions of the Institution of Naval Architects*, 44.

FAYOL, H. (1916). *Administration industrielle et générale* (Dunod and Pinat, Paris).

FLANDERS, A. (1964). *The Fawley Productivity Agreements: A Case Study of Management and Collective Bargaining* (Faber and Faber, London).

FLEURY, J. P. (1980). 'Les Brierons: essai d'approche d'une communauté ouvrière et rurale', Thèse du troisième cycle (Université de Nantes).

FLOUD, R. C. (1981). 'Britain 1860–1914: A Survey', in R. C. Floud and D. McCloskey (eds.), *The Economic History of Britain since 1700* (Cambridge University Press, Cambridge).

FORBES, S. and VARNEY, J. B. (1976). 'Ship Assembly Technology', in *Structural Design and Fabrication in Shipbuilding*, International Conference, London, 18–20 Nov.

FOX, A. (1985). *History and Heritage: The Social Origins of the British Industrial Relations System* (George Allen and Unwin, London).

FREEMAN, R. and MEDOFF, J. (1984). *What Do Unions Do?* (Basic Books, New York).

FRIDENSON, P. (1978). 'France, États Unis: genèse de l'usine nouvelle', *Recherches*, 32/33.

FYRTH, H. J., and COLLINS, H. (1959). *The Foundry Workers* (Amalgamated Union of Foundry Workers, Manchester).

GAMBETTA, D. (1987). *Were they Pushed or did they Jump? Individual Decision Mechanisms in Education* (Cambridge University Press, Cambridge).

—— (1988). 'Can we Trust Trust?', in id. (ed.), *Trust: Making and Breaking Cooperative Relations* (Basil Blackwell, Oxford).

GILLE, B. (1959). *Recherches sur la formation de la grande entreprise capitaliste, 1814–1848* (Sevpen, Paris).

GORDON, D., EDWARDS, R., and REICH, M. (1982). *Segmented Work, Divided Workers* (Cambridge University Press, Cambridge).

GRANT, A. (1950). *Steel and Ships: The Story of John Brown* (M. Joseph, London).

GRIPAOIS, H. (1959). *Tramp Shipping* (Thomas Nelson and Sons, New York).

GUIN, Y. (1976). *Le Mouvement ouvrier nantais* (Editions Maspero, Paris).

HAGAN, H. H. (1946). 'Shipyard Layout and Technique for Welded Construction', *Shipbuilding and Shipping Record*, 28.

HAIGH, B. P. (1933). 'Constructional Tests on Mid-Steel Rolled Sections with Electrically Welded Joints', *Transactions of the Institution of Naval Architects*, 75.

HALL, P. (1986). *Governing the Economy* (Oxford University Press, Oxford).

HANNAH, L. (1976). *The Rise of the Corporate Economy* (Methuen, London).

HARDY, A. C., and TYRRELL, E. (1964). *Shipbuilding: Background to a Great Industry* (Sir Isaac Pitman and Sons, London).

HARDY, J. (1951). 'L'Industrie des constructions navales en France', Thèse pour le Doctorat en Droit (Faculté de Droit, Université de Rennes).

D'HART, J. (1967). 'Extension en cours de réalisation aux Chantiers navales de la Ciotat pour la construction de navires de très gros tonnages', *Nouveautés techniques maritimes*.

HAYEK, F. A. (1986). 'The 1980s Unemployment and the Unions', in Coates and Hillard (eds.), *The Economic Decline of Modern Britain*.

HEINER, R. (1983). 'The Origin of Predictable Behavior', *American Economic Review*, 83.

HERON, A. (1975). 'Le Taylorisme hier et demain', *Temps modernes*, 31: 349–50.

HEY, J. D. (1981). 'Are Optimal Search Rules Reasonable?', *Journal of Economic Behavior and Organization*, 10.

HEYWOOD, C. (1976). 'The Rural Hosiery Industry of the Lower Champagne Region, 1750–1850', *Textile History*, 9.

HOGWOOD, B. (1979). *Government and Shipbuilding: The Politics of Industrial Change* (Saxon House, Farnborough).

HOLMES, G. C. V. (1906). *Ancient and Modern Ships* (South Kensington [now Victoria and Albert] Museum, London).

HOLMS, C. A. (1918). *Practical Shipbuilding* (Longmans, Green and Co., London).

HOSKYNS, SIR JOHN (1986). 'Mentioning the Unmentionable', in Coates and Hillard (eds.), *The Economic Decline of Modern Britain*.

HOULDCROFT, P. (1973). 'Steps in Welding Innovation and Achievement', *Metal Construction and British Welding Journal*, 5.

HUME, J. R. (1976). 'Shipbuilding Machine Tools', in J. Butt and J. T. Ward (eds.), *Scottish Themes: Essays in Honour of Professor S. G. E. Lythe* (Scottish Academic Press, Edinburgh).

JOHN, T. G. (1914). 'Shipbuilding Practice of the Present and Future', *Transactions of the Institution of Naval Architects*, 56.

JOHNSON, C. H. (1979). 'Patterns of Proletarianisation: Parisian Tailors and Lodeve Woollen Workers', in J. M. Merriam (ed.), *Consciousness and Class Experience in Nineteenth-Century Europe* (Holmes and Meier, New York).

JOHNSTON, T. L., BUXTON, N. K., and MAIR, D. (1971). *Structure and Growth of the Scottish Economy* (Collins, London).

JONES, L. (1957). *Shipbuilding in Britain: Mainly between the Two World Wars* (University of Wales Press, Cardiff).

JOSEPH, Sir KEITH (1986). 'Solving the Union Problem is the Key to Britain's Recovery', in Coates and Hillard, *The Economic Decline of Modern Britain*.

KALDOR, N. (1966). *Causes of the Slow Growth of the United Kingdom* (Cambridge University Press, Cambridge).

KEEBLE, D. (1976). *Industrial Location and Planning in the United Kingdom* (Methuen, London).

KEMP, T. (1962). 'Structural Factors in the Retardation of French Economic Growth', *Kyklos*, 15.

—— (1971). *Economic Forces in French History* (Dobson, London).

KENDALL, S. O. (1894–5). 'Turret-Decker Cargo Steamers', *Transactions of the North-East Coast Institution of Engineers and Shipbuilders*, ·11.

KENNEDY, W. P. (1976). 'Capital Markets in Britain to 1914', in L. Hannah (ed.), *Management Strategy and Business Development* (Macmillan, London).

—— (1987). *Industrial Structure, Capital Markets and the Origins of British Economic Decline* (Cambridge University Press, Cambridge).

KINDLEBERGER, C. P. (1964). *Economic Growth in France and Britain, 1851–1950* (Harvard University Press, Cambridge, Mass.).

KIRBY, M. W. (1981). *The Decline of British Economic Power since 1870* (George Allen and Unwin, London).

KIRKALDY, A. W. (1914). *British Shipping* (K. Paul, Trench, Trubner and Co., London).

KUSSE, J., and SLAVEN, A. (eds.) (1981). Proceedings of the September 1980 SSRC Conference on Scottish and Scandinavian Shipbuilding, University of Gothenburg.

LABROUSSE, E. (1966). 'The Evolution of Peasant Society in France', in E. M. Acomb and M. L. Brown (eds.), *French Society and Culture since the Old Regime* (Holt, Rinehart and Winston, New York).

LANDES, D. S. (1969). *The Unbound Prometheus* (Cambridge University Press, Cambridge).

LANGLOIS, R. N. (1986). 'Rationality, Institutions, and Explanation', in id. (ed.), *Economics as a Process* (Cambridge University Press, Cambridge).

LATTY, J. (1951). *Traite d'économie maritime*, i. *La Construction navale dans l'économie nationale* (Imprimerie nationale, Paris).

LAUX, M. S. (1972). 'Travail et travailleurs dans l'industrie automobile jusqu'en 1914', *Mouvement social*, 81.

LAVALÉE, L. (1919). 'Résultats obtenus par l'application des nouvelles méthodes de travail dans un chantier de 3000 ouvriers', *Bulletin de la société d'encouragement pour l'industrie nationale*, 118: 1.

LAZONICK, W. (1979). 'Industrial Relations and Technical Change: The Case of the Self-Acting Mule', *Cambridge Journal of Economics*, 3.

—— (1981). 'Competition, Specialization and Economic Decline', *Journal of Economic History*, 41.

—— (1986). 'The Cotton Industry', in Elbaum and Lazonick (eds.), *The Decline of the British Economy*.

LECLER, P. (1919). 'Réorganisation administrative des entreprises industrielles', *Bulletin de la société d'encouragement pour l'industrie nationale*, 118: 1.

LE MAISTRE, C. L. (1926–7). 'The Trade Value of Simplification and Standardization in the Details of Ships and their Machinery', *Transactions of the North-East Coast Institution of Engineers and Shipbuilders*, 43.

LEQUIN, Y. (1978). 'Labour in the French Economy since the Revolution', in P. Mathias and M. M. Postan (eds.), *Cambridge Economic History of Europe*, vol. vii, pt. 1 (Cambridge University Press, Cambridge).

LE ROY LADURIE (1970). 'Les Masses profondes: la paysannerie', in F. Braudel and E. Labrousse (eds.), *Histoire économique et sociale de la France* (Presses universitaires de France, Paris).

LEVINE, A. L. (1967). *Industrial Retardation in Britain, 1880–1914* (Weidenfeld and Nicholson, London).

LEVY-LEBOYER, M. (1968). 'Les Processus d'industrialisation: le cas de l'Angleterre et de la France', *Révue historique*, 92: 239.

—— (1976). 'Innovation and Business Strategies in Nineteenth- and Twentieth-Century France', in E. C. Carter, R. Forster, and J. N. Moody (eds.), *Enterprise and Entrepreneurs in Nineteenth and Twentieth-Century France* (Johns Hopkins Press, Baltimore).

LEWCHUK, W. (1987). *American Technology and the British Vehicle Industry* (Cambridge University Press, Cambridge).

—— (1989). 'Getting and Giving the Wrong Signals: The Decline of the British Motor Vehicle Industry', Paper presented at the Fourteenth Annual Meeting of the Social Science History Association Conference, November 1989; Washington, DC.

LITTLER, C. R. (1980). 'Internal Contract System and the Transition to Modern Work Systems: Britain and Japan', in D. Dunkerley and G. Salaman (eds.), *The International Yearbook of Organisational Studies* (Routledge and Kegan Paul, London).

LORENZ, E. H. (1981). 'The Labour Process and Industrial Relations in the British and French Shipbuilding Industries: The Interwar Years', in Kusse and Slaven (eds.), Proceedings of the September 1980 SSRC Conference.

—— (1984). 'Two Patterns of Development: The Labour Process in the British and French Shipbuilding Industries, 1880–1930', *Journal of European Economic History*, 13.

—— (1987). 'L'Offre de travail et les stratégies d'emploi dans la construction navale en France et en Grande-Bretagne, 1890–1970', *Mouvement social*, 138.

—— (1988). 'Neither Friends nor Strangers: Informal Networks of Subcontracting in French Industry', in D. Gambeta (ed.), *Trust: Making and Breaking Cooperative Relations* (Basil Blackwell, Oxford).

—— (1991). 'Trust, Community and Cooperation: Toward a Theory of Industrial Districts', in A. Scott and M. Storper (eds.), *Pathways to Industrialization and Regional Development* (Unwin Hyman, London).

—— and WILKINSON, F. (1986). 'The Shipbuilding Industry, 1880–1965', in Elbaum and Lazonick (eds.), *The Decline of the British Economy*.

McCLOSKEY, D. N. (1981). *Enterprise and Trade in Victorian Britain* (George Allen and Unwin, London).

McGoldrick, J. (1982). 'Crisis and the Division of Labour: Clydeside Shipbuilding in the Inter-War Period', in A. Dickson (ed.), *Capital and Class in Scotland* (John Donald and Co., Edinburgh).

—— (1983). 'Industrial Relations and the Division of Labour in the Shipbuilding Industry since the War', *British Journal of Industrial Relations*, 21.

McGovern, J. (1921–2). 'Some Notes on Shipbuilding Methods', *Transactions of the North-East Coast Institution of Engineers and Shipbuilders*, 38.

Marx, K. (1976). *Capital* (Penguin, Harmondsworth).

Matthews, R., Feinstein, C., and Odling-Smee, J. (1982). *British Economic Growth, 1856–1972* (Oxford University Press, Oxford).

Matthewson, S. (1969). *Restriction of Output among Unorganized Workers* (University of Southern Illinois Press, Carbondale, Ill.).

Mirowski, P. (1983). 'An Evolutionary Theory of Economic Change: A Review Article', *Journal of Economic Literature*, 17.

Montgomerie, J. (1937–8). 'Shipbuilding Practice Abroad', *Transactions of the North-East Coast Institute of Engineers and Shipbuilders,* 54.

Moore, B., and Rhodes, J. (1973). 'Evaluating the Effects of British Regional Economic Policy', *Economic Journal*, 82.

Morreaux, M. (1978). 'La Restructuration du secteur de la construction navale en France', *Économie et humanisme*, 240.

Mortimer, J. E. (1973). *History of the Boilermakers' Society* (George Allen and Unwin, London).

—— (1982). *History of the Boilermakers' Society*, ii (George Allen and Unwin, London).

Moutet, A. (1975). 'Les Origines du système Taylor en France: le point de vue patronale, 1907–1914', *Mouvement social*, 93.

Myerson, R. (1985). 'Analysis of Two-Person Bargaining Problems with Incomplete Information', in A. Roth (ed.), *Game-Theoretic Models of Bargaining* (Cambridge University Press, Cambridge).

Nelson, R., and Winter, S. (1975). 'Factor Price Changes and Factor Substitution in an Evolutionary Model', *Bell Journal of Economics,* 6.

—— —— (1982). *An Evolutionary Theory of the Firm* (Harvard University Press, Cambridge, Mass.).

—— —— and Schuette, H. (1976). 'Technical Change in an Evolutionary Model', *Quarterly Journal of Economics*, 90.

Nusbaumer, E. (1919). 'Essai d'application du système Taylor dans un grand établissement d'État (Pouderie du Ripault)', *Bulletin de la société d'encouragement pour l'industrie nationale*, 118.

O'Brien, P., and Keyder, C. (1978). *Economic Growth in Britain and France, 1780–1914: Two Paths to the Twentieth Century* (George Allen and Unwin, London).

OKAYAMA, R. (1979). 'Employers' Policy and Craft Unions: A Study of British Industrial Relations in Shipbuilding from the 1870s to the War', *Bulletin of the Institute of Social Sciences: Meiji University*, 2.

OLLSON, K. (1981*a*). 'Tankers and Technical Development in the Swedish Shipbuilding Industry', in Kusse and Slaven (eds.), Proceedings of the September 1980 SSRC Conference.

—— (1981*b*). 'Markets and Production in Swedish Shipbuilding', Discussion Paper for Gothenberg Conference on Shipbuilding History, 27–29 November, University of Gothenberg.

ORENSTEIN, H. (1944–5). 'Method and Motion Study applied to the Shipbuilding Industry', *Transactions of the North-East Coast Institution of Engineers and Shipbuilders*, 61.

OURY, L. (1973). *Les Prolos* (Éditions Denoel, Paris).

OWEN SMITH, E. (1971). *Productivity Bargaining* (Pan Books, London).

PARKINSON, J. R. (1956). 'Trends in the Output and Export of Merchant Ships', *Scottish Journal of Political Economy*, 3.

—— (1960). *The Economics of Shipbuilding in the United Kingdom* (Cambridge University Press, Cambridge).

PINCZON, M. (1930). 'Mission en Angleterre et en Écosse avec la délégation du Conseil national économique', Enquête du Conseil national économique, *Situation de l'industrie de la construction navale*, 1929–1930.

PLY, G. (1888). 'Étude sur l'organisation du service technique dans les manufacture d'armes' (extracted from the *Révue d'Artillerie*, Paris).

POLLARD, S. (1957). 'British and World Shipbuilding, 1890–1914: A Study in Comparative Costs', *Journal of Economic History*, 18.

—— (1982). *The Wasting of the British Economy* (Croom Helm, London).

—— (1989). *Britain's Prime and Britain's Decline: The British Economy, 1870–1914* (Routledge, Chapman, and Hall, London).

—— and ROBERTSON, P. L. (1979). *The British Shipbuilding Industry, 1890–1914* (Harvard University Press, Cambridge, Mass.).

PRECHEUR (1968). *Les Industries françaises à l'ère du marché commun* (Société d'enseignement supérieure, Paris).

PREST, A. R., and COPPOCK, D. J. (1982). *The UK Economy* (Weidenfeld and Nicolson, London).

PRICE, S. (1981). 'Labour Mobility in Clyde Shipbuilding, 1889–1913', Discussion Paper for Gothenburg Conference on Shipbuilding History, 27–29 November, University of Gothenberg.

Procedure Handbook of Arc Welding (1973). (The Lincoln Electric Company, Ohio).

PUECH, R. (1969). 'Évolution de la construction navale française depuis 1913', *Journal de la marine marchande*, 51.

RAPPING, L. (1965). 'Learning and World War II Production Functions', *Review of Economics and Statistics*, 48.

RAVAILLE, A. (1949). 'La Préfabrication en construction navale: son influence sur l'organisation et la production navale', *Bulletin de l'association maritime et aéronautique*, 48.

—— (1964). 'Le Planning en construction navale', *Nouveautés techniques maritimes*.

REDSHAW, L. (1947). 'Welding as applied to Shipbuilding', *Welding Research*, 3.

REID, A. (1980). 'The Division of Labour in the Shipbuilding Industry, 1880–1920, with special reference to Clydeside', Ph.D. thesis (University of Cambridge).

RICHARDSON, H. W. (1965). 'Retardation in Britain's Industrial Growth, 1870–1913', *Scottish Journal of Political Economy*, 12.

ROBERTS, G. (1967). 'Demarcation Rules in Shipbuilding' (Department of Applied Economics, Occasional Paper No. 14; University of Cambridge, Cambridge).

ROBERTSON, P. L. (1964). 'Shipping and Shipbuilding: The Case of William Denny and Brothers', *Business History*, 16.

—— (1975). 'Demarcation Disputes in British Shipbuilding before 1914', *International Review of Social History*, 20.

ROEHL, R. (1976). 'L'Industrialization française: une remise en cause', *Revue d'histoire économique et sociale*.

ROLT, L. T. C. (1971). *Landscape with Machines* (Longman, Edinburgh).

ROUX-FREISSINENG, M. (1929). 'L'Industrie des constructions navales en France', Thèse pour le Doctorat en Droit (Faculté de Droit, Université d'Aix).

RYAN, P. (1977). 'Job Training', Ph.D. thesis (Harvard University, Cambridge, Mass.).

SABEL, C., and ZEITLIN, J. (1985). 'Industrial Alternatives to Mass Production: Politics, Markets and Technology in Nineteenth Century Industrialization', *Past and Present*, 112.

SAMUEL, R. (1977). 'The Workshop of the World: Steam Power and Hand Technology in the Mid-Victorian Britain', *History Workshop Journal*, 3.

SANDBERG, L. G. (1981). 'The Entrepreneur and Technical Change', in R. Floud and D. McCloskey (eds.), *The Economic History of Britain since 1700*, ii (Cambridge University Press, Cambridge).

SARGENT, F. O. (1961). 'From Feudalism to Family Farms in France', *Agricultural History*, 35.

SAUL, S. B. (1967). 'The Market and the Development of the Mechanical Engineering Industries in Britain, 1860–1914', *Economic History Review*², 20.

SAVILLE, J. (1961). 'Some Retarding Factors in the British Economy before 1914', *Yorkshire Bulletin of Economic and Social Research*, 13.

SAXONHOUSE, G., and WRIGHT, G. (1987). 'Stubborn Mules and Vertical Integration: The Disappearing Constraint?', *Economic History Review*², 40.

SCHERER, F. M. (1975). *The Economics of Multi-plant Operation: An International Comparisons Study* (Harvard University Press, Cambridge, Mass.).

SCHIRACH-SZMIEGIEL, C. VON (1979). *Liner Shipping and General Cargo Transport* (Stockholm School of Economics, Stockholm).

SCHOTTER, A. (1981). *The Economic Theory of Social Institutions* (Cambridge University Press, New York).

SCHWARTZ, T., and VON HALLE, E. (1902). *Die Schiffbauindustrie in Deutschland und im Auslande* (Berlin).

SEROT, R. (1943). 'Armement et construction navale en France de 1914 à 1942', Thèse pour le Doctorat en Droit (Faculté de Droit, Université de Lyon).

SHEPHEARD, R. B. (1943–4). 'Recent Welding Developments in British Shipbuilding', *Transactions of the North-East Coast Institution of Engineers and Shipbuilders*, 60.

SHIELD, J. (1949). *Clyde Built: A History of Shipbuilding on the River Clyde* (W. Macmillan, Glasgow).

SILVERWRIGHT, G. W. (1888–9). 'The Development of the "Well-Deck" Cargo Steamer', *Transactions of the North-East Coast Institution of Engineers and Shipbuilders*, 5.

SIMON, H. (1957). *Administrative Behavior* (Free Press, New York).

SLAVEN, A. (1981*a*). 'Growth and Stagnation in British/Scottish Shipbuilding, 1913–1977', in Kusse and Slaven (eds.), Proceedings of the September 1980 SSRC Conference.

—— (1981*b*). 'Shipbuilding Industry Organizations and Policies 1920–1977', Discussion Paper for Gothenberg Conference on Shipbuilding History, 27–29 November, University of Gothenberg.

SMELLIE, J. (1923). *Shipbuilding and Repairing in Dublin: A Record of Work carried out by the Dublin Dockyard Co., 1901–1923* (McCorquodale, Glasgow).

STEARNS, P. N. (1978). *Paths to Authority* (University of Illinois Press, Urbana).

STEPHENSON, C. (1952). 'A Shipyard Reorganization for Welded Prefabricated Construction', *Transactions of the Institute of Welding*, 15.

STINCHCOMBE, A. L. (1959–60). 'Bureaucratic and Craft Administration of Production: A Comparative Study', *Administrative Science Quarterly*, 4.

—— (1960). 'Social Structure and Organizations', in J. G. March (ed.), *Handbook of Organizations* (Rand McNally and Co., Chicago).

—— (1986). *Stratification and Organization* (Cambridge University Press, Cambridge).

STONE, K. (1975). 'The Origins of Job Structures in the Steel Industry', *Review of Radical Political Economics*, 6.

STOPFORD, M. (1979). 'U.K. Cost Competitiveness' (Mimeo, British Shipbuilders, Newcastle-upon-Tyne).

—— (1988). *Maritime Economics* (Unwin Hyman, London).

STURMEY, S. G. (1962). *British Shipping and World Competition* (Athlone Press, London).

TERRY, M. (1977). 'The Inevitable Growth of Informality', *British Journal of Industrial Relations*, 15.

THEBAULT, P. (1979). 'L'Activité économique de la Basse-Loire de 1852–1939', Mémoire de Maîtrise (Université de Nantes).

TOLLIDAY, S. (1987). *Business, Banking, and Government: The British Steel Industry in the Interwar Years* (Harvard University Press, Cambridge, Mass.).

TUCKETT, A. (1974). *The Blacksmiths' History* (Lawrence and Wishart, London).

ULMAN, L. (1974). 'Connective and Collective Bargaining', *Scottish Journal of Political Economy*, 21.

URWICK, L., and BRECH, E. (1946). *The Making of Scientific Management*, ii. *Management in British Industry* (Management Publications Trust, London).

VAN DONKELAAR, A. (1932). 'Modern Dutch Shipyard Arrangement and Practice', *Shipbuilding and Shipping Record*, 39.

VAN PARIJS, P. (1981). *Evolutionary Explanation in the Social Sciences* (Rowman and Littlefield, Tobowa, NJ).

WALLACE, W. C. (1894–5). 'Electrical Transmission of Power in Shipyards', *Transactions of the Institution of Engineers and Shipbuilders in Scotland*, 38.

WEBER, A. (1961). 'Introduction', in id. (ed.), *The Structure of Collective Bargaining* (Glencoe, NY).

WHITE, W. H. (1899). 'The Connection between Mechanical Engineering and Modern Shipbuilding', *The Engineer* (5 May).

WIENER, M. (1981). *English Culture and the Decline of the Industrial Spirit, 1850–1980* (Cambridge University Press, Cambridge).

WILKINSON, F. (1973). 'Demarcation in Shipbuilding' (Department of Applied Economics Working Paper; University of Cambridge, Cambridge).

—— (1989). 'Industrial Relations and Industrial Decline: The Case of the British Iron and Steel Industry' (Department of Applied Economics Working Paper; University of Cambridge, Cambridge).

WILLIAMS, K., WILLIAMS, J., and THOMAS, D. (1983). *Why Are the British Bad at Manufacturing?* (Routledge and Kegan Paul, London).

WILLIAMSON, O. E. (1985). *The Economic Institutions of Capitalism* (Free Press, New York).

—— WACHTER, M. L., and HARRIS, J. E. (1975). 'Understanding the Employment Relation: The Analysis of Idiosyncratic Exchange', *Bell Journal of Economics*, 6.

WINTER, S. (1964). 'Economic "Natural Selection" and the Theory of the Firm', *Yale Economic Essays*, 4.

WOLFENDEN, F. T. (1976). 'The Submerged Arc Process in Shipbuilding', in *Structural Design and Fabrication in Shipbuilding*, International Conference, London, 18–20 November, The Welding Institute.

ZEITLIN, J. (1982). 'The Labour Strategies of British Engineering Employers, 1890–1922', in H. Gospel and C. Littler (eds.), *Managerial Strategies and Industrial Relations* (Heinemann, London).

Index